Digital Civics and Citizenship

Library Information Technology Association (LITA) Guides

Marta Mestrovic Deyrup, Ph.D., Acquisitions Editor
Core, a division of the American Library Association

The Library Information and Technology Association became part of Core: Leadership, Infrastructure, Futures, also a division of the American Library Association, in September 2020. Guides published in this series retain the series title LITA Guides.

The Library Information Technology Association (LITA) Guides provide information and guidance on topics related to cutting-edge technology for library and IT specialists.

Written by top professionals in the field of technology, the guides are sought after by librarians wishing to learn a new skill or to become current in today's best practices.

Each book in the series has been overseen editorially since conception by LITA and reviewed by LITA members with special expertise in the specialty area of the book.

Established in 1966 and integrated as part of Core in 2020, LITA provided its members and the library and information science community as a whole with a forum for discussion, an environment for learning, and a program for actions on the design, development, and implementation of automated and technological systems in the library and information science field.

Approximately twenty-five LITA Guides were published by Neal-Schuman and ALA between 2007 and 2015. Rowman & Littlefield and LITA published the series 2015–2021. Books in the series published by Rowman & Littlefield are:

Digitizing Flat Media: Principles and Practices
The Librarian's Introduction to Programming Languages
Library Service Design: A LITA Guide to Holistic Assessment, Insight, and Improvement
Data Visualization: A Guide to Visual Storytelling for Librarians
Mobile Technologies in Libraries: A LITA Guide
Innovative LibGuides Applications
Integrating LibGuides into Library Websites
Protecting Patron Privacy: A LITA Guide
The LITA Leadership Guide: The Librarian as Entrepreneur, Leader, and Technologist
Using Social Media to Build Library Communities: A LITA Guide
Managing Library Technology: A LITA Guide
The LITA Guide to No- or Low-Cost Technology Tools for Libraries
Big Data Shocks: An Introduction to Big Data for Librarians and Information Professionals
The Savvy Academic Librarian's Guide to Technological Innovation: Moving Beyond the Wow Factor

Digital Civics and Citizenship

An Applied Approach

Casey Davis

ROWMAN & LITTLEFIELD
Lanham • Boulder • New York • London

Published by Rowman & Littlefield
A wholly owned subsidiary of The Rowman & Littlefield Publishing Group, Inc.
4501 Forbes Boulevard, Suite 200, Lanham, Maryland 20706
www.rowman.com

Unit A, Whitacre Mews, 26-34 Stannary Street, London SE11 4AB

Copyright © 2021 by The Rowman & Littlefield Publishing Group

British Library Cataloguing in Publication Information Available

Library of Congress Cataloging-in-Publication Data

Name: Davis, Casey, author.
Title: Digital civics and citizenship : an applied approach / Casey Davis.
Description: Lanham : Rowman & Littlefield, [2021] | Series: Library Information Technology Association (LITA) guides | Includes bibliographical references and index. | Summary: "Regardless of age and experience, young adults must be mindful of their digital presence in the expanding digital world. This book provides a guide for librarians, educators, counselors, and administrators to guide secondary and higher education students in successfully practicing responsible citizenship and civics in the digital world"—Provided by publisher.
Identifiers: LCCN 2021000808 (print) | LCCN 2021000809 (ebook) | ISBN 9781538141342 (cloth) | ISBN 9781538141359 (paperback) | ISBN 9781538141366 (ebook)
Subjects: LCSH: Citizenship—Study and teaching. | Civics—Study and teaching. | Political participation—Technological innovations.
Classification: LCC LC1091 .D29 2021 (print) | LCC LC1091 (ebook) | DDC 370.11/5—dc23
LC record available at https://lccn.loc.gov/2021000808
LC ebook record available at https://lccn.loc.gov/2021000809

This book is dedicated to my wife, Raquel—my motivation for everything. Thank you.

Contents

Acknowledgments

This book would not have been remotely possible without the guidance and assistance of many people. The great thinkers and theorists I mention serve as the academic foundation for this work. As Sir Isaac Newton quipped, "If I have seen further, it is because I have stood on the shoulders of giants." This is also true in my experience. More importantly, I would like to thank those who have influenced and directed me in a more intimate way. The teachers, mentors, and counselors in my life challenged me not only to ask *why?* but to also respond *why not?* Their influence and encouragement continue to this day. The same is true of my family and friends, especially my parents. Those who claim me know who they are. Those who don't . . . well, we'll just politely nod to one another in passing. To both groups, I am eternally grateful. I also want to thank my students throughout my years of teaching. Your willingness to not only listen to my thoughts and ideas but also challenge them helped to bring this curious question of mine into fruition as a book.

A "shout-out" to my editor, Zuzana Urbanek at Z-Ink. If there are any errors, they are mine and mine alone. Z . . . you're awesome at what you do! I'd also like to thank Charles Harmon, Erinn Slanina, and the staff at Rowman & Littlefield. You not only took a chance on me but shepherded me through the publication labyrinth. My thanks also to the peer reviewers and beta readers. Your help goes further than you can imagine. Lastly, I want to thank my wife of almost thirty years. Raquel, your patience, love, and support have kept me going when nothing else would. Along with her, I want to give thanks to God for all the blessings of my life. May all that I do glorify you. Amen.

Introduction

What Is Digital Civics and Why Is It Important?

PURPOSE OF THE BOOK

This book is the product of my years of research, practice, and reflection as an educator and learner. Effectively guiding and assisting students in learning a body of knowledge or a set of skills requires understanding and appreciating the topic as its own entity. As more and more of my teaching practice migrated into the digital sphere (a territory that is relatively new to me but that I was and remain willing and eager to explore), the need to understand became paramount. Seeking to better understand the nature and need of digital civics and citizenship in education, I established a framework based on cognitive development for this study and the recommended methods.

The news reminds us daily of the negative impacts of social media. The psychosocial impact of both social media and the larger internet continue to make headlines in both popular media and academic journals. In fact, some national governments are calling the impact, especially on adolescents and young adults, an epidemic. It is difficult to argue against the influence and impact of social media on the overall mental health in Western nations. Evidence of this can be seen in the spate of suicides and shootings that regularly populate the daily news.

Until now, the majority of responses to mitigate these impacts have focused on equipping individuals with the tools to deal effectively with their emotions in response to social media posts or digital attacks. These efforts include an increased discussion and focus on building internal strengths such as resiliency. Similarly, the K–12 spectrum of education, including home-schooling, has adopted a renewed zeal concerning social-emotional learning and development.

However, there is a different perspective. While building resiliency and a certain sense of toughness is vital to personal success, there is more to individuals that just these aspects. People are multidimensional, and this needs to be respected in education at all levels and in all contexts. So it is necessary to increase the significance of individual perspectives.

The approach advocated in this book seeks to add the attributes of respect and advocacy, balancing between internal and external points of view, to the current trends of striving to instill a sense of resiliency and mental toughness within individuals. Using the traditional understanding of civics and citizenship practice and education, this book moves forward with the best practices provided by this tradition. These best practices are identified, explored, and closely examined in this book.

These best practices, however, are not blindly adopted and implemented in the approaches recommended in this book. A certain amount of adaptability is needed. The practices must embody flexibility and continue to evolve into the future to maintain their relevance. But in some ways these practices are based on fundamental, universal truths regardless of an individual's particular worldview.

INTENDED AUDIENCE

The audience for this book is found in three primary groups: K–12 educators and administrators, higher education instructors and administrators, and librarians in the public and academic realms. This book also helps educators connect with parents and guardians/caregivers. Of course this does not limit readership by other individuals who may not fit neatly into the above-mentioned categories. In fact, this book is open to a wide audience.

There are only two prerequisites. First is some individual experience with digital technology. It's probably safe to say that the majority of folks living and breathing fit into this category. Second is to have a little bit of curiosity.

Perhaps curiosity should have been mentioned first. Even without any experience or knowledge of the digital world, everyone is part of a community, whether it is a formalized community or an ad hoc organization of individuals. People are all members of such groups. Even the hermetical monastic is a member of a religious community. As such, we are all bound by a framework, both explicit and implicit, that governs our daily lives, interactions, and activities, however mundane they may seem.

This framework provides a lot of fodder for thought and reflection. In fact, it can be the source of many questions, and even frustrations from time to time. The questions of why we live under rules, where the rules come from, and who has the authority to create, enforce, and interpret them are age old. These questions often lead to more questions rather than answers.

However, sometimes the questions themselves are more important than the answers.

Simply put, this book is for anyone and everyone living today. It is challenging and at times confusing enough trying to navigate the social mores and legal confines of our real lives, and adding a digital dimension only compounds these feelings. However, the objective of this book is to provide insight and perhaps some hope based on the important role that civics and citizenship play in society. These aspects of civilization and society are interesting in themselves. Civics and citizenship can be understood as organisms that are both pushed down by structures of authority as well as pushed up from the proverbial grassroots level of individuals in a society.

Unlike traditional, or corporeal, society, the digital realm is expanding exponentially on a daily basis. Wars, conquests, and economic forces are not the primary drivers of the cybersphere.

In fact, this nascent realm of existence is primarily dependent upon individual use. This in itself is a curious state of affairs for the end users, we humans. It's almost as if the digital realm is expanding at the speed of thought. The task of organizing a workable set of guidelines for interacting with one another within the cybersphere can seem impossible. However, together we can make this seeming impossibility into a virtual reality.

SCOPE OF THE BOOK

Understanding and appreciating the foundations upon which the approach and methods found in this book are built is crucial. Our current interest in digital civics and citizenship is nothing new. Removing the "digital" aspect from the topic, civics and citizenship have fascinated us collectively and individually since family groups evolved into clans, tribes, villages, and then societies and civilizations.

Ever since the formation of groups of nonbiologically related individuals, and perhaps even before then, humans have wondered why some individuals rose to leadership positions while others did not. Similarly, people have struggled to understand what it means to be a member of a particular group. This is especially true when it comes to special privileges and responsibilities bestowed on members. Members and nonmembers, insiders and outsiders, myself and others, are all existential binaries that continue to serve as the axis around which civics and citizenship revolve.

The first section of the book looks at the origins of civics and citizenship, as well as our understandings, practices, and transmission of these aspects of civilization from antiquity to current times. It identifies the good that has come from these practices and understandings in an effort to transfer and adapt them to modern usage. Similarly, it points out parts that need to be left in the past. They should not necessarily be forgotten. To do so would risk repeating them, with perhaps worse results.

This section of the book ends with a look at how civics and citizenship education is embedded in K–12 education through an evaluation of the current learning standards, as well as how it is communicated within the realms of higher and community education. Alongside this examination, this part of the book also addresses learning outcomes in these three areas of education concerning computer and digital technology.

From this vantage point, the gaps in teaching and learning are identified. This provides the necessary bridge to the second section of the book. This section provides some recommended approaches to teaching digital civics and citizenship within the mentioned areas of education. It also provides some proposed improvements to these areas to strengthen digital civics and citizenship education.

The second section is devoted solely to tried and tested best practices that educators can employ. Some of the approaches and methods shared are appropriate for specific learner populations, while others are easily adapted across the learning continuum. Most importantly, none of the methods or approaches provided in the text are turnkey.

As with any educational endeavor, educating individuals in digital civics and citizenship is a dynamic and organic undertaking. Just as people grow and adapt to their circumstances and our understanding of the brain through the various sciences continues to grow, these methods and approaches must be flexible. When they are, this makes the experience engaging and authentic, giving the method or approach a longer life span compared to one that is rote and heavily formulaic.

The key attribute these learning experiences share is just that: experience. Aside from the foundational knowledge of civics and citizenship, the recommended learning experiences in the second portion of the book are experiential in nature. Given the nature of digital civics and citizenship, experiential learning is perhaps the best, if not the only logical, approach to teaching it.

Many of the experiences incorporate best practices from other content areas and methods of education and training. In fact, some readers may recognize similar experiences and activities from other subject areas, grade levels, and courses they have either taught or journeyed through as a participant. More than anything, the flexibility of these experiences is key to cultivating engagement through improvisation on the part of the facilitator along with the participants.

Improvisation is the key to authentic learning experiences. Just as crucial, improvisation is at the heart of digital civics and citizenship. Given the human basis of this context, it comes as no surprise. It is also key in the final portion of the text.

The third section of the book explores some of the possible pieces through which individuals can show working mastery of digital civics and citizenship. As in the second section, the products recommendations are flexible and adaptable. This flexibility is necessary to make the products authentic for the audiences using them. Again, these recommended products are neither exhaustive nor definitive. They are ones that have been incorporated into a variety of settings with a variety of participants and have resulted in success through positive results.

COVERING NEW GROUND

There are ways in which this book covers new ground or presents a different perspective. Even though digital civics and citizenship is something of a nascent subject, its roots reach back to antiquity, and there are quite a few works currently available that explore this topic.

The majority of these texts, journals, and other pieces focus on the topic itself. These works closely examine what digital civics and citizenship are and the role technology plays. They are all important facets of digital civics and citizenship. They are vital not only for understanding and practicing digital civics and citizenship, but also for appreciating this dynamic and organic topic as experienced in our daily lives, often without our being conscious of it.

Given this reality, questions arise concerning how someone learns to be a digital citizen, what constitutes digital civic virtue and works, and many other practical issues. So this book makes a concerted effort to address these questions of education and application. Before the term *application* misleads anyone, know that the applications, methods, and approaches to teaching and learning digital civics and citizenship are grounded in scientific research. The methods and approaches for providing authentic and engaging learning experiences in this book rely on research-based best practices. In other words, the activities and experiences are ones borrowed from current educational practices, but the content being taught is different.

The parts of this book concerned with practice and products, which takes up two-thirds of the text, are recommendations. As stated earlier, these approaches and products are ones that have been developed within the learning experience. They are shared in the hopes of adoption and adaptation. They are not strict rules or recipes for delivering reproducible results. The aim of exploring and learning digital civics and citizenship is not to produce cookie-cutter citizens. The goal is to equip individuals with tools and inform them how best to navigate and operate in the digital sphere.

REAL PRODUCTS

The one facet of this text that stands out perhaps more than any other is the supply of recommended learning activities and experiences. These recommendations are products of years of teaching a diverse population of students across a variety of contexts. However, that's just the superficial understanding of the uniqueness of this text. More lies beneath.

This book opens an exciting realm of possibilities and probabilities. This book is key for exploring and expanding the world of digital civics and citizenship in a very real and practical nature. The recommended learning experiences and activities provide learners with the opportunity to enter not only into the topic itself, but also into a dynamic and organic virtual community where they can have a direct impact on the community's evolution.

At the time of writing this text, there is no other book offering anything like this. There are some texts that share similarities, but most focus on the topic of digital civics and citizenship as a concept rather than as a practice. This book flips the focus. However, it also balances this approach with a solid grounding in the tradition of holistic teaching.

While learning outcomes can be quantitatively measured, the majority of results are more qualitative in nature. Individuals will be able to witness but also help create a blossoming of respect, community, and advocacy online between one another. Now, this is not a claim that reading this book and following its recommendations will automatically make someone a better citizen or change an entire community. This book is not in any way a magic cure. It's not a proverbial silver bullet for correcting what some find wrong in society today. The book does, however, provide some tools for reshaping and reforming our digital society in a way that is respectful of all individuals involved.

BACKGROUND INFORMATION

As mentioned, this book relies not only on decades of scientific research in cognitive development, developmental psychology, and educational methodology, but also on centuries of philosophical examination of the nature of civics and citizenship, especially the relationship between the individual and the community.

This book grew out of curiosity. Most learners' earliest experiences of growing up include being instructed in patriotism at home and at school. During this time, students read and parse, as much as they can, the founding documents of the United States of America. In fact, each one of us had to memorize and recite the preamble to the Constitution. Rote? Rigid? Traditional? Yes, to all of these.

This book is founded on some of the traditional approaches to civics and citizenship education, but it does not stop there. Using the latest research-based methods and pedagogies, it puts examples, tools, and learning experiences into the hands of educators for adoption and adaptation to their unique teaching contexts. Don't let these traditional actions keep you from reading and finishing this book. It will soon become apparent that these are just "first steps" in a greater journey in teaching and learning digital civics and citizenship.

Part One

Foundation

Chapter One

Overview

There are two primary takeaways intended for readers of this book. Both are measurable. The first is attaining and mastering digital civics and citizenship to at least a working-level competency of the knowledge and skills contained within this topic. The other, grander objective is focused on community. It is hoped that, through the exploration and application of the knowledge and skills embodied in digital civics and citizenship, participants will actively engage in building a healthy and vibrant community, cultivate an existing community, and serve as guides to new members of these communities by teaching, showing, and practicing digital civic virtue and the attributes of a good digital citizen.

Readers of this book will gain understanding and a deeper appreciation of civics and citizenship through the experience of these within the cybersphere. Unlike traditional civics and citizenship, the actions and attributes are not necessarily transferrable without a certain amount of evolution and adaptation.

ORGANIZATION

This text is organized in a way that guides readers through a defined progression. Each section builds upon the foundation provided by the previous section. The second and third sections offer a branched organization that allows focus on specific portions, as the learning activities and experiences are grouped by audience: K–12, higher education, and community education.

Readers can easily skip over the parts that do not address their particular audience without necessarily losing context or flow within the overall work. However, the experiences and outcomes examined in other portions should not be ignored. Given the right context and perspective, they could be adapted to fit other audiences.

The first section is the foundation of the entire work. Essentially this first part explores the significance of digital civics and citizenship. It aims to answer the question *why?* This single question is perhaps the most important. With any undertaking, one must be able to answer why it is important to expend the time and effort doing it. We need to know why we are doing something in order to give the act meaning.

This first section attempts to address the why of digital civics and citizenship by examining the philosophy and psychology of civics, citizenship, and community. As mentioned, the perspective in this book reaches back to antiquity to incorporate classical Greek, Roman, and Chinese societies and philosophies regarding civics and citizenship. These form the essential foundation for incorporating traditional understandings and practices within the cybersphere. Of particular importance in constructing this foundation is the Greek concept of *eudaimonia*, or regard for the individual and one's respective community, the city-state in this particular instance.

The next essential component is the Roman understanding of citizenship and civic virtue. Given the fact that much of Western society and civilization continues to build upon the legacy of the Romans, it is essential to understand and appreciate how their society informs and influences our current understanding and practice of civics and citizenship. In doing this, it is possible to glean those aspects and attributes that are fundamental and transferrable to the digital realm.

Next, the first section examines the impact Confucianism played in shaping classical Chinese society in regard to educating individuals in civics. Even today, Confucianism continues to influence the ordering of society in modern China. Confucianism is different from other schools of civics and citizenship in antiquity because of its dual focus on the individual's relationship to the state and to other individuals. This is compared to Greece and Rome, where the focus in civics and citizenship was on the relationship between the individual and the state.

Leveraging Confucianism's dual perspective provides a crucial part of bridging from traditional civics and citizenship into the cybersphere.

From this classical perspective, the first section progresses to a brief examination of traditional civics and citizenship education. The K–12 civics and citizenship education in the US public school system is used as a case study. While experiences differ from state to state and from nation to nation, this experience was selected because it was the one I have personally experienced in my educational journey. As such, it is one case study explored in this book.

The first section finishes with a look at the foundational and seminal works of developmental and cognitive psychologists. Their theories influence and inform the practices and products provided in the subsequent sections of the book. The work of great thinkers such as Piaget, Buber, Fromm, Bandura, and Vygotsky provides more than just a theoretical framework for teaching digital civics and citizenship. Their work also establishes a path to follow through the mystery of the human mind, its workings, and human behavior at different stages and ages of individuals who populate our audiences. From the work of these researchers have evolved best practices for teaching and learning. This is the scientific support for the methods and approaches offered in this book. The following chapters are in the first section:

What Is Civics?—This chapter explores the idea and concept of civics in both the Western and Eastern traditions. This chapter explores the philosophical and psychological foundations of civics. This examination secures the traditional understandings of civics to build upon them later in the text.

What Is Citizenship?—This chapter explores the idea and concept of citizenship in both the Western and Eastern traditions and the philosophical and psychological foundations of citizenship. This examination secures the traditional understandings of citizenship to build upon them later in the text.

What's Been Done in the Past—This chapter examines and analyzes how civics and citizenship are currently being taught, especially in K–12 and higher education. Within this chapter, the focuses, standards, and expected outcomes are incorporated using state and federal learning standards.

Where Do We Go from Here?—This chapter examines and analyzes how technology is currently being taught, especially in K–12 and higher education. Within this chapter, the focuses, standards, and expected outcomes are incorporated using state and federal learning standards.

Social-Emotional Learning and Cultural Literacy —This chapter examines the current high-value focus on social-emotional learning and pairs it with the theory and practices of cultural literacy from the 1980s. This synthesis provides an approach to address the individual needs of learners while cultivating a positive culture in learning digital civics and citizenship.

Virtue Ethics and Digital Civics and Citizenship—This chapter builds on the previous one to identify those methods and experiences that are based on a traditional understanding of ethics and ethics education adapted to the digital realm. Specific approaches, methods, and experiences for learners are explored in greater detail in the second part of the chapter.

The second section of the book provides some examples of practice for learning digital civics and citizenship. *Praxis*, the root cognate of *practice*, is the Greek term for "act." More specifically, *praxis* in this text is used to address the so-called gap between theory and product. This section is focused on putting theory into practice to achieve a particular outcome. As with any educational or instructional practice, a certain amount of flexibility and latitude must be expected. People are individuals, not widgets. Centuries of failed educational experiments continue to show that learning is not a rote, cookie-cutter operation. It is incumbent on the learning leader to adapt the method to best engage the student.

This section is divided into three focuses: K–12, higher education, and community education. At the beginning of each is a brief explanation of the intended audience and suggested context. As stated, these should be taken as guidelines. All of the learning experiences provided in this section can be adapted, for the most part, for audiences other than their suggested one. Achieving this is up to the instructor.

One possible way to read this section is sequentially, regardless of your intended audience. In doing so, it will become apparent that even within this section the learning experiences are divided to a certain extent. The context of these experiences becomes less restrictive as the audience members age and progress through different cognitive developmental stages. For example, teaching a student in elementary school what it means to be a citizen is going to look different than it might in a community center or public library with a group of adults. The methods differ in accordance with the audience, but the message remains the same. Following are chapters in the second section:

Approach to Teaching Digital Civics and Citizenship—This chapter serves as a bridge between the first two sections, transitioning from theory and history to modern practice. Adapting techniques from other disciplines and content areas is explored in order to ease the implementation of this approach in a variety of contexts.

Diversity, Inclusion, and Equity in Digital Civics and Citizenship—This chapter applies the evolving focus on diversity, equity, and inclusion to the realm of digital civics and citizenship education, revealing how these two approaches actually complement and build off each other.

Teaching Digital Civics and Citizenship—This chapter explores the "how" of teaching digital civics and citizenship in three settings: K–12, higher education, and community education. Practical experiences and guidance for instructors are provided in this chapter.

Integrating with the STEM/STEAM Curriculum—STEM education is currently a major focus of discussion and practice, with no hint of fading anytime soon. As more attention and funding become attached to STEM, it is only natural that digital civics and citizenship will become integrated with it. More importantly, these two areas are complementary, even though this seems counterintuitive upon first glance.

Integrating Digital Civics and Citizenship with a Traditional Curriculum—Authentically instructing participants in digital civics and citizenship means that these topics must be embedded within the current, established curriculum. This is especially true in the K–12 and higher education realms. Doing this provides learners with the opportunity to see digital civics and citizenship as part and parcel of learning and living rather than as add-ons.

This chapter provides some suggested approaches and methods to achieve this.

Stand-Alone Learning Experiences—This chapter provides a sampling of learning experiences appropriate for the different contexts focused on throughout this text. These experiences contain information and activities for learners, as well as notes and suggestions for instructors. Each of these experiences has measurable learning objectives. Suggested assessments and measurements are included as well.

Sample Lesson Plans and Learning Activities—This chapter offers an overview of a suggested curriculum framework. Also included are examples of ready-to-use lesson plans and learning activities. This is primarily for instructors, administrators, and organizations looking at adopting an entire curriculum for digital civics and citizenship. This is not a complete overview but rather a sample of what could be done to evaluate or create a curriculum.

Standards, Outcomes, and Objectives —This last chapter of the section examines selected federal learning standards and how embedding digital civics and citizenship within learning experiences addresses those standards. Along with this analysis, a brief overview demonstrates how to deconstruct a learning standard to help gain a deeper understanding of the embedding process.

This book provides a starting point for conversations and collaborations. For example, say a K–12 campus or district adopts these practices. Leaders from this organization can reach out to a local college or university as well as the local community and share this resource to approach the issue from as holistic a perspective as possible.

Readers can focus solely on a particular spectrum of intended audience and only read that part of these two sections. The outcomes will not differ substantially. However, even if other entities do not enter into a collaborative learning partnership, reading through the text sequentially can still help provide educators with additional ideas and possibilities that only need modification for their particular audience.

Anyone familiar with education of any type realizes that the process has multiple parts. The third and final portion of this book is titled Products. The surest way for learners to practice their newly acquired knowledge and skills as well as to show attainment of the expected level of mastery is through products. In traditional educational settings, these products include tests, reports, and other assigned work. However, for the purposes of this book, products are different, based on the nature of the content knowledge and skills as well as the context in which they are being taught.

The majority of the recommended products provided in this text are experiential. This is crucial for two reasons. Developmental psychology continues to provide evidence that humans are strongly influenced by their experiences. As such, providing learners with controlled, or "safe," situations in which to experience and learn is paramount. This means that the products are not necessarily traditional. As a result, measuring outcomes proves to be challenging, as they rely on an ad hoc mixture of qualitative and quantitative measurements. This is starkly different from the more traditional and recognized products that can be easily measured quantitatively. Following are chapters in the third portion:

Products and Assessments—This chapter explores the ways in which an instructor can measure and assess learners' progress and achievement. The framework of social-emotional learning anchors this exploration. Examples of quantifiable and qualitative measurements are provided for assessing the learning experience.

Cultivating Culture—This chapter features an exploration of the impacts of digital civics and citizenship education on the classroom as a community. The framework of social-emotional learning anchors this exploration. Examples of quantifiable and qualitative measurements are provided for assessing the learning experience.

Looking Ahead—The goal of this chapter is to provide not only a perspective but also hope for the future of virtual community building through digital civics and citizenship education. This chapter balances a dual point of view by paying respect to the past and providing hope for the future.

Resources—This final portion of the book provides readers with ready-to-use resources for teaching digital civics and citizenship. These resources include organizational websites and activities, as well as learning standards and objectives.

As with any work of educational practice, readers must keep in mind one real truth while exploring the practice and its processes. The methods, approaches, and activities provided in the text are *not* a magical potion or proverbial silver bullet. This book does not provide a broad-spectrum cure-all for the classroom. However, it does offer tips, tricks, and tools to educators for authentically implementing and engaging students in digital civics and citizenship education. The time and effort needed to adapt and implement this method and its constituent activities not only provides tangible results but also long-term products that extend outside of the learning environment and into the larger community.

Chapter Two

What Is Civics?

Civics is an aspect of life that most people believe they know about, and some do. The term is tossed around nonchalantly in government and politics regularly, and usually incorrectly. Sadly, this often leads to a misunderstanding of civics and its denigration in popular conceptions. An understanding of the term and the methods shared in this text may serve to help citizens themselves to remedy and repair this situation.

The simplest definition of *civics* is "the collection of the actions and body of knowledge concerned with the rights and responsibilities of citizens." However, the seeming simplicity of this definition should serve as a warning to the depth and complexities that churn underneath like riptides. The currents and tides are navigable with a proper map. This text will serve as a map to help learners and educators navigate these shifting tides.

For the purposes of this exploration, *civics* does have to do with the body of knowledge and the collection of actions expressing citizens' rights and duties within a nation, vis-à-vis the current government. In this way, civics is understood as a relational condition of existence defined by the individual to the whole.

This existential and phenomenological perspective comes from a famous adage from Aristotle, who said, "For the things we have to learn before we can do them, we learn by doing them." Aristotle presented this interesting turn of a phrase in his work *Nicomachean Ethics*.

This singular foundation is the impetus for Sudbury schools, which began offering K–12 education in the late 1960s. These schools teach and operate on the idea of direct democracy. By definition, direct democracy is also known as pure democracy, in which individual citizens have direct influence on governmental policies. Sometimes the Athenian style of democracy from classical times is provided as an approximate example. Direct democracy is not to be confused with representative democracy, which is the form most commonly practiced.

- In that work, as well as in his *Eudaimonia Ethics*, Aristotle explores and examines the topics of ethics and politics, controversial even in his day. Linguistically, the root word of *ethics* is *ethos*, which is understood to mean "character," as in the spirit of a community or era, or, in a more modern sense, the acts and beliefs of an individual. During Aristotle's time, much as in ours, the development of character was understood as a deeply personal and intimate undertaking.

Aristotle was the first philosopher to study and examine the topic of ethics in depth. For his intents and purposes, ethics was concerned with what is considered beautiful or just. This in itself is challenging since beauty is very much in the eye of the beholder in regard to current sensibilities. In Ancient Greece there was more of a shared understanding of beauty. So the question arises as to how one can arrive at something resembling a unified or shared definition of beauty and what is just.

Essentially, both of Aristotle's treatises focus on generating and cultivating *eudaimonia*, which can be understood as "flourishing." Aristotle's primary objective was not merely to instruct individuals on how to conduct themselves within society but, more importantly, to use these individual acts and behaviors to construct a society in which individuals can flourish, thus allowing the culture to flourish as well.

During Aristotle's lifetime, Greek culture held that *eudaimonia* was the highest and noblest goal a person could strive for and possibly attain. In a certain sense, Aristotle's point of view was to examine and understand the relationship between individual acts and cultural evolution and refinement. Likewise, a refined culture and a flourishing society impact the evolution of its constituent members.

Aristotle identified three ways, or means, of flourishing for an individual. The first, considered the lowest form, was to thrive through physical pleasures. This seemingly slavish means of "flourishing" was understood by many as the route to achieving happiness. On the other end of the spectrum, the third, or highest, means to achieve flourishing was through prolonged meditation and contemplation. This lofty route was not functionally viable for the majority of individuals since it required an economic security that few had then, and few have today.

The second route, or middle way, to flourishing was through a refined and active political life. It was via this route that Aristotle believed individuals could achieve honor. At this time, the Hellenistic culture believed that a person attained honor through intelligence, wisdom, and judgment. Politics, Aristotle purported, was the best means of exercising these three virtues.

So, one way to understand this is that politics is not only an honorable endeavor for individuals to undertake in life but also one that is necessary.

Aristotle posited that individuals who undertake politics help to keep society in some sort of balance between the capricious desires and whims of the mob, or the hoi polloi, and what is best for the state or society overall. Some scholars point to these two works by Aristotle as the transition from direct to representative democracy within Greek society, and in the classical world in the larger sense.

Aristotle went further to explore the idea of civics in his foundational work *Politics*. In this book, Aristotle addresses the idea of both moral virtue, *arete* in Greek, and what would come to be known as civic virtue, *ethos*, expanding upon the earlier definition of the term. Later, during the Roman Republic, these two terms would be combined in an ad hoc understanding called *virtus*. Both the Greeks and the Romans understood that individual citizens had certain responsibilities in the civil society of which they were members. These duties ensured that the civil society not only continued to function but was fortified and evolved.

In essence, this perspective of civics and civic virtue can be understood as the relationship of a part to the whole. Like an organism composed of a variety of different cells, each cell has a specific function to perform. However, given the fact that humans have the attribute of agency, or free will, the dilemma is how to induce individuals to work for the common good.

For Aristotle and the Greeks, education and enlightenment provided the means.

Essentially the Hellenes understood that civic virtue was based on honor. Honor continues to be something of a tricky aspect of existence and being. Debates still live on about honor's nature, necessity, and negative impacts. For better or worse, the last dimension of these discussions seems to be in the majority in the current times. In our current times, *honor* is both praised and ridiculed, as it is often confused with hubris, or pride.

Understanding this, the term *civics* comes to mean a relationship between an individual and society—a part to a whole, if you will. This is vital not only in understanding civics for our journey but also in appreciating the different points of view on citizenship that will be shared later.

From Aristotle, we leap forward to the Enlightenment. The "big three" of the seventeenth and eighteenth centuries—Hobbes, Locke, and Rousseau—provide further understanding of the nature of civics and citizenship, civic virtue, and the roles these play in a society. Drawing from classical Greek and Roman philosophies as well as canon law, social contract theory has helped to shape democratic societies and continues to influence their evolution.

Social contract theory is a foundational current within societies throughout the world. It influences almost everything. Economic exchanges, political discourse and policy, public education, and organizations such as homeowner associations are all inheritors of this school of thought. Similarly, this theory can greatly inform digital civics and citizenship.

Just as social contract theory informs and influences physical societies and communities from the current understanding, it can also guide and facilitate digital societies and communities. In fact, it already has to a certain extent. Ironically, there is something very natural and biological about the transference of the social contract, and all its trappings, from conventional society to the digital realm.

As more and more individuals from democratic societies become active in the digital realm, they bring with them certain expectations about organization and behaviors online. This is known sociologically as expectancy theory. This theory describes the motivation of an individual's choice of behavior as being influenced by expected results or rewards.

Simply put, as we venture into the digital realm, we expect to encounter and engage other individuals in a similar fashion to how we do so in the real world. The level of respect, countenance, and even register of speech expected and used online is influenced, and sometimes dictated, by the experiences we bring with us. Behaviors, attitudes, and actions are carried over, for better or for worse.

However, navigating and engaging in the digital realm has unique challenges. Unlike communicating across communities and cultures in the physical world, time and distance no longer serve as borders or even identifiers in the digital realm. It is commonplace for individuals around the world to communicate, collaborate, and challenge each other easily.

Engaging with others online is governed by different psychological influences than traditional, face-to-face exchanges. Traditionally, individuals have had time and distance to make a transition, to raise their awareness of being in a different place, with a different culture, or cultures. Even without time and distance, the ability to observe and judge facial expressions and body language facilitates a better understanding of the message being communicated. Without this dimension of communication, messages are misunderstood, and meaning can be miscommunicated.

Just as civics and citizenship can provide a framework for social communication and interaction in the physical world, they can provide this guidance in the digital world. The interaction between individuals online, however, demands some adjustments and adaptations.

Traditional civics and citizenship education could be easily considered "nationalistic," and for good reason. Often, civics and citizenship were taught as an indoctrination rather than an education. Yet this does not diminish the methods and means used in teaching the content knowledge and skills to participants. Of course, the major change in teaching digital civics and citizenship would be in the point of view.

Unlike traditional civics and citizenship education, digital civics and citizenship education needs to guide participants to becoming productive citizens within the digital realm by practicing responsible digital civics. National boundaries are now literally reduced to just lines on a map. National and political identities hold only as much weight or meaning as the participants want them to.

While this liberates individuals from many preconceived notions and limitations that have to be overcome in face-to-face communication, it also allows participants to virtually reinvent themselves online. Unfortunately, this is not always their truest self. In fact, many people purposely reinvent themselves online given the level of anonymity the cybersphere offers. In some instances, these acts are used to defraud and harm others. Since the advent of the internet and the continuing expansion of the digital realm, the news has been replete with stories of individuals who have been harmed and worse by individuals who have pretended to be someone else online.

While this particular challenge is multifaceted and deserves a multifaceted solution, it is essential to understand that digital civics and citizenship is one of those facets. Establishing a framework of conduct and communication for individuals to practice helps to cultivate expectations organically.

This is the way it should be: expectations and processes in a community should be organic and dynamic in nature. This provides the opportunity for a community and, on a larger scale, a society to evolve within the digital realm. Doing so provides the latitude needed for communities and a society to take shape in a way that is similar to the physical world. Digital civics and citizenship education can help champion human rights, civil liberties, and other facets of democratic societies.

UNDERSTANDING CITIZENSHIP AND CIVICS

Whether wading into this realm through philosophy, practice, or producing good citizenship practices and civic societies, one needs a clear, delineated differentiation between *citizenship* and *civics*. They are distinct from one another, even though they can work in tandem. Identifying the unique attributes of citizenship and civics helps to recognize and appreciate how these two complement and cultivate each other in practice and influence one another in understanding.

As will become more apparent as you keep reading, the philosophy, teaching, and practice of digital citizenship and civics can be strongly informed by traditional citizenship and civics education and practice. The philosophical underpinnings for digital citizenship and civics hark back to classical Greek and Roman philosophies, plus other sources from ensuing ages, which offer a wealth of understanding and guidance.

Citizenship

One of the best and easiest ways to understand citizenship is by focusing on the individual. Citizenship encompasses the individual rights and civil liberties an individual has as a citizen of a particular nation or state. This is the essence of what is meant when someone states, "I am an American" or "I am a Mexican" or other similar statements. At their heart, such statements are political in nature. However, there are social and cultural trappings that go along with these political statements. The understanding and appreciation for rights and liberties such as freedom of speech, right of assembly, and other civil liberties as enumerated and recognized in the Bill of Rights are present, at least for a US perspective. These rights are not merely transferrable to the digital realm but are alive within the cybersphere.

Civics

Different from but complementary to citizenship, civics takes the perspective of the larger group, the society in which an individual is a citizen. Civics encompasses the rules and responsibilities that citizens, residents, and visitors are expected to abide by and exercise while in a nation, state, or country. Civics is how citizenship is shown. Civics is the acts and actions of an engaged and active citizenry.

Examples of this in the United States are actions such as voting, participating in civic holidays, working for the good of the community, and other acts. To fully practice civics, an individual must have a working knowledge of what it means to be a citizen, especially living in a society of citizens who share the same rights and responsibilities, realizing that these may be expressed in diverse ways.

Combining these specific understandings of citizenship and civics, as well as how they complement each other, brings up the question of what citizenship and civics look like in the cybersphere. How are they understood? How are they practiced? What do they mean for individuals exercising their digital existence online?

There are no easy answers to these vital questions regarding digital citizenship and civics. Perhaps the greatest challenge that must be recognized and grappled with is how an individual, or a group of individuals, can claim citizenship in cybersphere. Then, once citizenship is established and recognized, how do digital communities and societies form and evolve? This then introduces the questions of how rules, regulations, ordinances, and laws are created. Who enforces them? Who adjudicates infractions?

Trying to stem the tide of cyberbullying and other online attacks, as well as the challenge of protecting individuals online, may seem insurmountable as technology continues to grow and flourish. However, it is in facing these challenges and grappling with the opposition to digital civics and citizenship education that these questions become more manageable, and perhaps where some possible solutions for teaching digital civics and citizenship arise. Some possible solutions will be explored later in this book.

Chapter Three

What Is Citizenship?

The relationship between civics and citizenship is vital. Without citizens and their individual embodiment and practice of citizenship, civics would remain an abstract idea. A good idea, no doubt, but it would remain inert. It is up to each individual participant to take it off the shelf and practice it to collectively create a vibrant community. With the ubiquitous nature of technology, the majority of the world's population are now citizens of the digital world. As a result, the need for a framework of relational communication and behavior is needed, such as digital civics and citizenship.

Citizenship is defined as the position and privileges an individual holds by being a legally recognized subject or resident of a certain nation or country. This is the political position occupied by a citizen. When individuals claim or exert their citizenship, they are claiming the rights, rules, and responsibilities of being a part of a particular nation, country, or community.

For the purposes of this examination, digital citizenship will have its own distinct meaning. Its understanding certainly draws from traditional definitions and functions as well as philosophical understandings, but adaptation is necessary to ensure that citizenship may be a viable, vibrant, and regular part of the digital sphere.

Citizenship in the digital sphere is a beguiling facet of existence, of being. It challenges us all to understand an added dimension of existence in cyberspace that continues to evolve and inculcate itself into everyday life. In fact, in most of the developed world today, to not have a digital presence is to make a conscious decision to remove oneself from this dimension of existence. However, the very nature of existence in the digital sphere proves challenging when trying to define and use traditional understandings and perspectives.

Digital existence is virtual by nature. As such, an individual's profile, personality, and presence online are purely dependent on that person's choices. Similar to individuals who wear "masks" in the physical world, people in the digital sphere have a much easier time creating their psychological masks and convincing others of their veracity. While this is an obstacle in the physical world with interpersonal relationships and interactions, it is an even greater challenge online. Without the assistance of body language, facial expressions, and voice inflections, individuals online have a greater need for "playing it smart" when it comes to evaluating their interactions.

Learning and practicing good citizenship, particularly online, goes quite a long way in keeping the experience pleasant and productive as well as helping to ensure individual safety. By looking at digital citizenship through a dichromatic lens, balancing the hues of alien citizen and natural citizen as espoused by Bosniak,[1] the robust and beguiling virtual reality of digital citizenship becomes apparent.

In the "natural citizenship" form and function, individuals in most cases operate within a set of standards and expectations that already exist a priori to the individual. These expectations, attitudes, behaviors, and actions are passed down from one generation to another. Traditionally, this is done from parent(s) to child(ren). However, in the digital sphere, it occurs somewhat differently.

In the digital realm, every individual is equal in a certain sense. The internet has leveled the playing field. Simply put, it has flattened our world. Thomas Friedman has provided a great framework for understanding this recent phenomenon in his book *The World Is Flat*. Using this paradigm, the internet is the great equalizer. On the flip side, it is an amorphous entity that can be easily swayed and directed. It might be helpful to think of this aspect of the internet as something akin to the all-consuming Blob that came into the world in the 1958 B movie.

As a result, the challenge of establishing a just society based on mutual respect in the digital sphere is similar to the economic and philosophical dilemma known as the "tragedy of the commons." In this sense, the unregulated nature of the internet can feed the rapacious and greedy side of many people. This mechanistic and Darwinian understanding incites the fears of individuals and societies. It is the root of many misunderstandings in the digital realm. In a sense, it positions the digital sphere as the proverbial wilderness, one filled with menacing shadows and fearsome unknowns.

Yet this proverbial wilderness can radiate possibilities. Connections to be made, edifices to construct, and discoveries to celebrate may be waiting just beyond the virtual tree line.

Without falling into the trap akin to Manifest Destiny, a certain cathedral can be constructed in this wilderness. Like the settlers who physically moved west, this construction will take many hands. In fact, it must be done communally in order to last. No one individual can build this structure, or it would not be an organic society.

Primarily, the goal of this book is to help individuals grow and evolve into responsible and respectful digital citizens. Likewise, the expectation is that these digital citizens will cultivate digital civics and civic virtue among the ever-expanding society within the digital realm. To accomplish this, educators must strike a balance, ever precariously, on the proverbial razor's edge.

Regardless of teaching context, educators play a pivotal role socially, educationally, and politically. K–12 teachers are familiar with this terrain. Teachers working in this context are legally understood as in loco parentis. Legally, this means that teachers are responsible for their students as parents would be in other circumstances. They are charged with guiding and assisting their students.

This seems fairly simple and innocuous, but there is more to it, especially in regard to citizenship. Teachers are officially charged with instructing students in their assigned content areas at a particular grade level. What has faded from expressed responsibilities, to something akin to subtext, is the responsibility of helping students to become good and productive citizens.

There's the rub. Unlike in decades and centuries past, teachers today aren't allowed to overtly teach students how to behave per se. Teachers can share, instruct, and guide practice for students regarding their behavioral expectations. These are taught within the context of the classroom. Once mastered, they can be used as points of reference for students in making decisions regarding actions and reactions outside the classroom.

This may seem obfuscated. However, in practice, it is clear that K–12 classroom teachers can instruct students on behaviors and actions only as long as it is tied to classroom interactions. Examples of this range from something as simple as learning to line up or raising a hand for a question to as complex as working together in a laboratory setting or engaging in a civil debate. In a certain sense, this means that classroom teachers can provide something akin to ethical instruction. Yet the teaching of moral virtue remains solely the responsibility of parents and guardians, as well as religious representatives from various faith traditions. The law has established this.

It is with this understanding that we may better appreciate the phrase "it takes a village." In the traditional sense, teachers are crucial in raising and developing young individuals into adults. Yet it can be generally agreed that this aspect of responsibility has overtly diminished publicly since about 1960 for various reasons. The one reason most regularly pointed to by social and educational researchers is the countercultural movement.

Taking this presupposition as a given for the purposes of this text, teachers have to juggle these legal constraints in order to fulfill the unwritten social and political expectations associated with their role. With this in mind, this text aims to provide a framework for doing so in the K–12, higher education, and community education contexts. A nimble juggling of these educational responsibilities can work in a legal sense and, more importantly, bring about positive learner-centered results.

Simply put, teachers *can* instruct and guide students in becoming active and respectful citizens who embody and practice civic virtues and maintain authentic respect for the individual context of each student. This is a major goal of any education. Doing so respects the individual and the collective history and culture of students while educating them, stoking the fires of nascent curiosity embodied in us all.

Citizenship encompasses all teaching and learning. The philosophy and practice of digital citizenship is relatable to every content area and discipline in the academic realm. The different elements of citizenship comfortably and authentically reside within many of the academic skills taught in the K–12 classroom, expand in the higher education environment, and level off in the realm of community education.

For example, one of the staples of learning mathematics is showing your work. This provides evidence to the teacher of the students' different thinking processes. In essence, showing the work in solving a math problem reveals the train of logic utilized to arrive at the answer, hopefully the correct one. A skilled classroom teacher will have the student walk through their thinking in solving the problem. Doing so allows the student to see what they did correctly and where errors may have been made. In a certain sense, this is an act of self-discovery.

Researching, crafting, and drafting a persuasive or informative paper for an English class, or an analysis paper for a history course, provides a similar experience for students. Under the guidance of a mentor, the teacher, they examine and question their thinking and logic used to analyze and communicate a topic or opinion. The same is true for the arts. Whether it is about notes and tones, hues and shadows, or movement and gestures, students are guided by their teachers to examine their choices and actions in light of what helps them arrive at solutions and insights.

By analyzing the logic, teachers can guide students in making choices that are civic minded, respectful, and responsible without necessarily impinging upon their individual rights and liberties. Like a classical, liberal education, instructing students in digital civics and citizenship is at its foundation a journey through critical thinking. This strikes at the heart of all education, which is guiding students to recognizing the fact that we are all mortal. With this realization, teachers assist students in identifying how they can live a meaningful and productive life. This was the undercurrent that flowed throughout chapters 7 and 8 of Aristotle's *Politics*.

Similarly, it was revisited further in his less well-known work *Laws*.

An American cultural anthropologist, Ernest Becker,[2] wrote extensively on the topics of death and meaning. Becker understood these two as being inextricably linked to one another. In his seminal work, *The Birth and Death of Meaning*, Becker posits that if humans undertake something of meaning, something larger than themselves, they will strive to generate a legacy and turn from the pessimism and nihilism of realizing the existential truth of our own individual demise. In general, individuals want to leave a legacy for the future that is positive and even inspiring to others. With this understanding, educators at all levels and in all contexts are encouraged to not merely pass along content knowledge and skills to students, but to guide and assist them in creating meaning. Perhaps nothing can be more civic-minded or serve as the foundation for being a good citizen than this understanding. And this lies at the heart of the importance of digital civics and citizenship.

Helping an individual discover meaning in their life provides a foundation for learning and practicing digital civics and citizenship. The understanding that they are a part of a larger whole, and that their acts and behaviors impact the group, is not only a realization of responsibility but also provides added depth to meaning. So educators should appreciate the great role they play in teaching. It's not just an exercise in communicating content, but in a larger sense it is assisting learners in discovering and making meaning.

NOTES

1. Linda Bosniak, *The Citizen and the Alien: Dilemmas of Contemporary Membership* (Princeton, NJ: Princeton University Press, 2008).

2. Ernest Becker, *The Denial of Death* (New York: Free Press, 1997).

Chapter Four

Current State of Civics and Citizenship Education

According to the Center for American Progress, seventeen states currently require students to pass a citizenship test in order to graduate from high school. Similarly, forty states require students to take and pass a civics course of some sort. In many states, this is embedded within one of the social studies requirements. Along with this, in thirty-one states the civics course contains what is referred to as "a full curriculum."[1] More on this last part a little later.

Regardless, civics education continues to be, at least statistically, a fundamental part of K–12 education. The Brown Center Report[2] published by the Brookings Institution reveals similar data. While this may seem to provide a sense of relief in regard to reports of flagging civics education, exit polls from all levels of elections reveal a less-than-optimistic point of view in regard to the practice of civics, otherwise known as citizenship in general. In other words, we're teaching the rules of engagement, but people seem to be following them less all the time.

This disparity has led many political pundits and policy analysts to place the blame squarely on the shoulders of public education. Sadly, these accusations may not be too far from the truth. Many news reports and talk shows provide evidence that the "man on the street" is neither very knowledgeable nor conversant in what would be considered civics and citizenship. Again, education becomes the primary scapegoat in this situation.

As education plays a primary role not only in creating this situation but also in alleviating it, the weight of responsibility cannot be laid entirely upon K–12. The realms of higher education and community education must bear their fair share of responsibility as well. Doing so produces its own unique set of challenges. For example, all levels and forms of education must respect the agency of an individual, but there is still some responsibility on the educational entity of instructing said individual. Even so, these challenges and opportunities are interrelated and articulated upon one another, something akin to Russian nested dolls.

For example, the Middle States Commission on Higher Education (MSCHE) has specific criteria for institutions that are either accredited by this body or are seeking accreditation that parallel the practices and philosophy of digital civics and citizenship. Under their Standard 2, the commission states the following:

> An accredited institution possesses and demonstrates the following attributes or activities:
>   1. a commitment to academic freedom, intellectual freedom, freedom of expression, and respect for intellectual property rights.
>   2. a climate that fosters respect among students, faculty, staff, and administration from a range of diverse backgrounds, ideas, and perspectives. [3]

However, MSCHE, as well as other accrediting institutions, does not specifically provide examples of what this would look like in any particular context. One of the aims of this book is to address this gap to assist and guide learning organizations in applying digital civics and citizenship.

In higher education, the debate between factions either supporting outcome-based education, answering the question of "What are you going to do with your degree?" or supporting a traditional, liberal educational experience that teaches students how to learn still rages. Given the ever-skyrocketing cost of attending an institution of higher education—and no, it's not just the cost of tuition—and the more competitive job market awaiting graduates, students are becoming savvier consumers. In doing so, colleges and universities have had to adapt in balancing what their students/customers want with what they need in order to be professionally and personally successful.

Traditional staples of an undergraduate education such as the humanities and arts have been usurped by the social sciences, by courses listed under "preprofessional studies," and so forth. As a society, it cannot be expected that a shift to a focus on attaining a job postgraduation will not impact the traditional liberal curriculum in higher education. As arguments and debates orbit around this lack of instruction, some see it as wholly necessary in order that students not be indoctrinated into a particular political philosophy or government party. While this is not necessarily an unfounded fear, it seems as though citizenship and civics education have gone the way of the proverbial bathwater.

This leaves community education as something akin to the final bastion. However, a quick review of offerings provided by local public libraries and community centers leaves much to be desired. Accordingly, classes, workshops, and assistance offered in these settings exist only to help citizens understand issues, hear candidates speak, and learn where their local polling stations are located—functional information at best.

In light of these understandable strictures, public educational organizations face a difficult road to travel in regard to citizenship and civics education. However, digital civics and citizenship education is not impossible. In fact, it aligns quite nicely with the established educational standards that all K–12 students, teachers, and administrators are held to, and that higher education students are expected to have mastered. Essentially, to teach students how to think critically, to scrupulously examine policies and platforms, to respectfully engage publicly, and endeavor to keep informed about issues, citizenship and civics education will continue to be cultivated. Similarly, when this is expanded into the digital sphere, constructive and collaborative growth will also be experienced. Yet the key is to build upon what already exists.

FOCUSES

Given the previous section, it is not difficult to surmise the current focuses within existing citizenship and civics education. These include the branches of government, how federalism works, a brief history of American government, major court cases and decisions that shaped the evolution of the federal government, and voting laws. Usually a cursory examination of the Declaration of Independence, the Constitution, and the Bill of Rights is included as well. This content knowledge is all well and good. It is foundational knowledge. However, rarely is it built upon, expanded, or cultivated.

Similarly, computer education is wholly focused on student use. Participants learn how to successfully navigate and implement the tools available through most operating systems. However, there is little critical or philosophical reflection and exploration of these tools, as well as their uses. Again, there is little wrong with including this knowledge and skills within computer education curricula. Like the framework for citizenship and civics education listed above, these points are amazing pieces upon which to found a curriculum.

There is further to go.

Even in the military, recruits are just taught how to use a weapon, in most cases a rifle, as well as its upkeep, but perhaps more importantly, when to use it, how to gauge the need for its use, and other knowledge to build upon. In other words, recruits are taught how to think through situations they may face when armed so that the use of deadly force is applied correctly. Words and ideas are no different. They must be handled with care and concern. Improperly used, they can hold their own unique lethality.

This particular approach to citizenship and civics education proposes not just a blending or enfranchisement of these two content areas, but also expansion of their scope and depth. This can be achieved without impinging upon an individual's civil liberties. The key to accomplishing this type of educational experience is utilizing case studies in a seminar-type atmosphere where students are assisted in reaching their own conclusions through critical reasoning. There is not a set or expected answer. Students are expected, rather, to support their answer and "show their work" by sharing the logic they used in arriving at their answer or decision.

For the purposes of digital civics and citizenship education, an amalgamation of existing standards across different disciplines and content areas provides educators and students with the road map necessary to become active and engaged digital citizens adding constructively to this new realm of existence. These expanded expectations are built on the existing foundations located within the K–12 realm, adapted for the diversity of audiences expected, and expanded to include amorphous skills such as critical thinking, public discourse, and research.

CRITICAL THINKING

Critical thinking is one of the continuing hallmarks of compulsory education. Many individuals, both public and private citizens, bemoan the growing lack of it in the populace. Education policy makers seek to build it into all realms of education. The rest of us are still befuddled as to what critical thinking is, how to teach it, and how to measure it. For our purposes, we will use the following understanding provided by the Foundation for Critical Thinking:

> Critical thinking is the intellectually disciplined process of actively and skillfully conceptualizing, applying, analyzing, synthesizing, and/or evaluating information gathered from, or generated by, observation, experience, reflection, reasoning, or communication, as a guide to belief and action. In its exemplary form, it is based on universal intellectual values that transcend subject matter divisions: clarity, accuracy, precision, consistency, relevance, sound evidence, good reasons, depth, breadth, and fairness. [4]

The examination of critical thinking is further expanded by the foundation to note that critical thinking resides within other forms of looking at and analyzing the world, such as mathematical and scientific thinking, along with philosophical and moral thinking, as well as a host of others. In other words, critical thinking is not only instantiated within these realms of thinking, but axiomatic and essential.

Similarly, the Foundation for Critical Thinking identifies two primary aspects of critical thinking. These are, "1) a set of information and belief generating and processing skills, and 2) the habit, based on intellectual commitment, of using those skills to guide behavior."[5] In other words, critical thinking's ultimate goal is to understand. For the purposes of this exploration, this understanding is the foundation upon which action and opinion are based. Essentially, the aim of civics and citizenship education is to assist and guide participants to becoming an informed electorate. More on this in the coming sections.

STANDARDS

Educational standards are something of a touchstone subject in the current social atmosphere. The purpose of this exploration is not concerned with the nature and generation of educational standards, especially in regard to civics and citizenship education. There are numerous well-informed volumes of research and analysis on this particular subject. For our purposes, the adoption and adaptation of existing standards inform and concern us. Within the realms of higher and community education, there are few standards. Yet certain academic and professional organizations have established professional ethics and standards to govern the daily operations and research undertaken by members. However, it takes a stretch of critical and creative thinking faculties to extrapolate learning standards from these.

Whether on the state or federal level, civics and citizenship learning standards are embedded within existing social studies standards that students, teachers, and administrators are assessed by on an annual basis. However, in response to the Next Generation Science Standards, the National Council for Social Studies released its own revised version of standards to help bring social studies education, including civics and citizenship education, into the twenty-first century. Standards are good and have been adopted and adapted by many state departments of education. Yet the purview of these standards only encompasses K–12 education.

The different bodies of learning standards can be leveraged successfully to generate a framework for implementing this initiative and successfully engaging individuals in order to guide and assist them in becoming positive and productive digital citizens. This framework needs to be flexible enough to change with social contexts as they ebb and flow through time, as well as providing the latitude for adaptation and evolution. While I advocate the creation of a set of standards to assist and guide citizenship and civics education at all levels, there is some hesitancy for generating something that would become restrictive and ossified. Only time will show how the nation, society, culture, and the world progress. However, a framework is needed to assess progress and mastery as an individual journeys through the digital civics and citizenship educational experience, as well as to provide some sort of guaranteed standardization of results.

OUTCOMES

As mentioned, the outcome of successful digital civics and citizenship education is to produce an informed citizenry that is authentically and respectfully engaged in civic activities. Individuals who have reached a certain level of mastery in critical thinking cannot be easily categorized.

These results of successful digital civics and citizenship education are an ad hoc mixture of behaviors, attitudes, and actions. For example, an individual who has mastered digital citizenship and civics up to an operational, or applied, level engages respectfully with others online, as well as in person, who have differing opinions and perspectives. Similarly, the individual advocates for others, especially when they are being treated in a disrespectful manner, regardless of the context. Lastly, an individual who has attained this level of mastery in digital civics and citizenship endeavors not merely to persuade others to accept their perspective or understanding on a topic or issue, but to educate them in regard to the logic and thought processes used to arrive at that particular opinion.

The educational aim of digital civics and citizenship does not come to completion in persuading a disagreeing individual but moves further. It also includes seeking to understand a different and perhaps foreign understanding and perspective on a particular topic or issue. In this sense, digital civics and citizenship education assists in guiding an individual to attaining their "protean self."

Realizing this also reveals the continuing conundrum in learning and development. Teachers, administrators, and even parents and guardians cannot guarantee or dictate how an individual in their charge will think, politically, philosophically, or otherwise, once they have attained legal majority according to their chronological age. They can only hope that the newly minted adult will use the tools of critical thinking and analysis in making decisions. One truth about education that can help not just in accepting this but in celebrating it as reality is keeping in mind the end goal of education. This has been worded in a variety of different ways, but the truth of the matter remains. The goal of education is not to teach what to think. Rather, as Jean Piaget wrote, "the goal of education is not to increase the amount of knowledge but to create the possibilities for a child to invent and discover, to create men who are capable of doing new things."[6]

NOTES

1. https://cs4.socialstudies.org/resourcesmain/new-item4/new-item.
2. https://www.brookings.edu/series/brown-center-report-on-american-education.
3. https://www.msche.org/standards/#standard_2.
4. http://www.criticalthinking.org/pages/our-mission/405.
5. Ibid.
6. Kathe Jervis and Arthur Tobier, eds., *Education for Democracy: Proceedings from the Cambridge School Conference on Progressive Education* (Weston, MA: Cambridge School, 1988).

Chapter Five

What's Been Done in the Past

After a glimpse of previous and current civics and citizenship education, it may be understandable why a deep-seated fear has developed. The idea of enculturating, and sometimes indoctrinating, students to citizenship through civics education has morphed from its original, well-meaning driving force. Waves of indoctrination fear have ebbed and flowed throughout the history of nations. History bears witness to the impact of these tidal rhythms.

Originally, civics and citizenship education focused on ensuring that students understood their rights and responsibilities as citizens of their nation. National holidays, famous leaders, civic history, and the evolution of the nation were sprinkled throughout the curriculum.

Expectations for students were laid out, including learning about the sacrifices made by those who founded the state along with those who were active in its cultivation and evolution. The desired outcome was for learners to take up the mantle of citizenship, with all its responsibilities, and carry on the work of conservation and cultivation of the state into the next generation. Likewise, learners who mastered the content and skills were expected to support and pass along this body of tribal knowledge to their progeny.

Decades later, after two world wars, this realm of education took on a new dimension of seeming indoctrination. The Cold War heightened the ideological boundaries between East and West, and questioning democracy or contemplating communism was tantamount to treason. This is understandable, given the geopolitical situation at the time. With time providing distance, it has become apparent that this hypernationalism blocked critical thinking among students exploring citizenship and civic virtue. These components of education and social enculturation cannot be ignored or forgotten without grappling with the result, which includes apathy and indifference.

This is the current state found in society and needs to be addressed in the realm of K–12 education. Low voter turnout, hyperpartisan response to politics, and a collapse of civil discourse and action are all symptoms of the pulling away from incorporating citizenship and civics education. Understanding this path helps us to appreciate the centrality and necessity of civics and citizenship education.

The specters of Henry Ford, nationalism, McCarthyism, and other menacing entities from the past can overshadow the future of this type of education and its positive effects. However, they can also serve as lessons to be learned, internalized, and leveraged in order to not repeat past mistakes.

The history of civics and citizenship education does provide some key tools and a solid foundation to build a framework for digital civics and citizenship education. As with most endeavors, dogged vigilance ensures not falling into familiar patterns while making progress.

The evolution of technology, specifically computer education, is a bit easier to reflect upon given the relative "newness" of the tools and the fairly straightforward approach to technology education. Given that computer and technology education evolved from what was previously referred to as business and vocational education, it is not surprising that this focus continues to guide students to successfully master the use of these tools, which are now digital.

Yet, even in the early days of technology, education lacked an attempt to answer the question of *why*. Students rarely think of the machines and applications they learn to use as powerful tools. These tools can be utilized to create and destroy. Unlike typewriters, computers with word-processing programs and applications are able to create documents and other products that can exist in perpetuity, for all intents and purposes. Documents created, statements shared, and other means of communication in the digital sphere reside on a server or in the cloud until purged, and even then traces can be recovered with the use of other powerful cyber tools. This means that anything created on a computer or mobile device can be accessed without the originator, or "owner," providing permission or even being aware.

Also, digital communication has removed the "presence," or physical aspect, of interpersonal communication. This is not necessarily negative in itself, but this aspect of communication is crucial in obtaining a proper understanding of a message. Being able to read the sender's body language, tone, and voice inflections provides a deeper understanding and appreciation of the message. With the rapidity and ubiquitous nature of digital communication, especially through social media, this aspect is often missing and results in miscommunication—no matter how many emojis appear.

Currently, the only tangible approach to civics and citizenship education and training can be found in the K–12 area. It is more often than not led by counselors within schools. While these efforts do not necessarily focus on digital communication, citizenship, or civics, counselors focus on social-emotional learning to help students cultivate resilience, respect, and reflection in interpersonal relationships. As has often been the case, such educational efforts are now siloed, thus fracturing students' understanding and perspective.

Previously in public education, civics and citizenship instruction was very rote, with little discussion of the topics included in the curriculum. Activities included memorizing the preamble to the Constitution and one or a handful of the amendments, identifying civil liberties in the Bill of Rights, and other similar exercises. There was little time or attention given to unpacking these items or the philosophy and history behind them.

In higher education, requirements that students take a government course deepen this study from K–12, comparing the philosophy of government to its current practice at the local, state, and national levels. Some students may also have opportunities to compare the governments of different nations. However, little if any attention is given to civic responsibilities outside of voting and paying taxes.

The same holds true with community education. Unless a group facilitates an instructional meeting on a proposition, bond issue, or something similar, most learning experiences focus on registering to vote and locating the correct polling stations for individuals.

It is not necessarily the nature of students attending public junior high schools or retirees participating in a community learning group at a public library to want to do a deep dive, unpacking the layers behind America's republic and its democratic processes. Yet this doesn't mean that these groups, as well as others, can't participate in discussions on these issues. Many times, if educators capitalize on the opportunity, they will more often than not be surprised with the results. Students of any age are curious about why things are the way they are. In fact, one way of igniting learners' curiosity is by partially answering their questions. This builds on the established Socratic method, but in an equitable and conversational manner.

Looking at civics education throughout the twentieth century, it seems it's been left behind. The progress of education becomes apparent, while the evolution of civics education content and methods remains curiously stagnant. Here's an excerpt from *Elementary Civics* by McCarthy, Swain, and McMullins published in 1916:

> Self-government is easy in the family, because the group is small. Father, mother, and the older children can come together to talk things over. It is harder for the city, because it is more difficult for its citizens to come together to talk things over. It is still harder in a nation. The ancient Greeks learned how to let all the free men of the city take part in the government of the city so long as their number permitted them to assemble in one meeting place. The Romans founded a larger state than the Greeks had done, and they were unable to work

out a plan by which all the free men of the empire could take part in governing themselves. In many cities of the Roman Empire the free men governed, but that was the extent of democracy in the Roman Empire.

Since it was so difficult to have self-government in a large state, how does it happen that although the world is being united into larger and larger states, these states are growing more democratic? [1]

The language used in this brief passage discussing self-government reveals the historical context in which elementary-level students were taught civics. The fact that women's enfranchisement as evident in the right to vote had not been recognized federally in the United States must be kept in mind when reflecting on this passage. From a twenty-first-century perspective, it is ironic given the fact that digital technology has been used as a great emancipator as well as a great segregator in the world.

Here is an excerpt from *Civics and Citizenship: A Sourcebook for Schools*, published in Canada in 1961 for assisting teachers in the K–12 spectrum:

As an ethical faith, democracy is premised on certain universal values or ideals of the good life. In some respects these values or ideals are analogous to the rules of a game. In any organized game the rules define how the game ought to be or should be played. They thus give purpose and direction to the game. The rules provide the players with a common basis for what it means to win; they make team play possible. At the same time, they provide the referee or umpire with a standard by which to evaluate the behaviour of the players during the game. For, although the rules describe how a certain game ought to be played, they do not describe how the game is being played at any particular moment. Players may, and often do, break the rules. Penalties may have to be assessed against a team or an individual player. [2]

Even though this text was published in Canada for use in Canadian public schools, the sentiment is complementary to that expressed in the textbook utilized in public schools in the United States almost half a century earlier. It is interesting that democracy, according to the authors of this particular text, can be understood and expressed as a type of faith. Again, from a current perspective, this is somewhat ironic given that the majority of democratic nations pride themselves on a clear and present separation of church and state.

However, taking a longer perspective on civics and citizenship education, the practice of civic virtue and the embodiment of citizenship was seen as something akin to divine with the classical Greeks and Ancient Romans, particularly during their republican periods in history. Thousands of years later, these texts are evidence that a faint current of these sentiments was still coursing through Western democracies in the world.

Even as the majority of Western democracies continue to separate church and state to great lengths, the idea that civics is a form of secular, state-oriented religion haunts this course of study. In many ways, the instructional approach has matched the tenor of the content.

Civics has been traditionally taught in a fairly strict and formal way. Students were expected to memorize particular portions of founding documents, recite the Pledge of Allegiance, and know requisite dates and names from the revolutionary and early national periods in the United States. Even at the cusp of the new millennium, civics and citizenship education had not evolved much from a century before.

> Project '87, a joint effort of the American Historical Association and the American Political Science Association, is proud to sponsor this book, *Lessons on the Constitution*, for students, teachers, and curriculum developers. The Lessons are an integral part of Project '87's program on behalf of the Constitution's Bicentennial. They are meant to be supplementary instructional material that can be easily adapted by teachers for use by their students in classes on civics, American history, and American government. Additionally, this book is a resource for other organizations and individuals engaged in efforts to enhance teaching about the Constitution. The Lessons were prepared in order to meet the need for more instruction on the United States Constitution, its history and theory.[3]

Interestingly, just by reading and reflecting on these few excerpts from civics and citizenship educational texts, a few shared characteristics become evident. These excerpts show the vitality and significance of the founding documents of these nations. In the United States, these are most often the Declaration of Independence and the Constitution. Canada also has its constitution. Both nations owe a huge debt to England's Magna Carta. Just comparing and contrasting this fact between these two geographically massive nations that share the same continent is a deep and complex discussion. These similarities, shared by other nations as well, are a powerful foundation to open digital communication between people around the world.

As exemplified in these excerpts, the evolution in the educational materials for students in the United States shows that the focus was on educating well-informed and engaged citizens. Ideas of civic virtue and social responsibility were norms within the curriculum. However, as the understanding and practice of public education adapted with the times, the focus narrowed to surveying the founding documents and discussing the voting process, the branches of government, their responsibilities and jurisdictions.

As a result, any type of social-emotional learning all but disappeared from civics and citizenship education in the United States. In some ways, this is ironic given the current trend in public education. One could even contend that the increasing recognition of the importance of social-emotional learning, along with the adoption of curricula supporting this, may be an effect of removing this portion from civics and citizenship education.

The primary arguments used to support the removal of social education and training from public education have already been listed. The arguments for removing social-emotional learning from public education, especially in civics and citizenship instruction, could possibly be circumvented effectively by approaching the learning experience in a different way. The proposed approach, explored in greater depth later in the book, builds on the traditional instruction of language arts.

In one aspect of language arts instruction at the secondary level, along with communications courses in higher education, students learn about the different registers of language that are appropriate in various situations. They range from formal (used for academic papers, business letters, and so on) to informal (used in familiar speech and notes) and have several permutations based on different sources. Digital civics and citizenship can leverage this foundation and add to it.

Since the primary objections to incorporating ethical and moral education within civics and citizenship instruction are couched in maintaining civil liberties, approaching that instruction from a linguistic standpoint of register seems both logical and as unobjectionable as possible. With this understanding, learning and practicing digital civics and citizenship is not much different from effectively communicating with a diverse audience in a variety of contexts.

As will be explored in more depth in a later chapter, combining social-emotional learning with digital civics and citizenship instruction allows educators and students to explore ethics in a virtual environment to make it as respectful of individual perspectives and choices as possible.

By doing so, students have opportunities for participants to learn and relearn most suitable behaviors to engender civil communication behaviors in a safe space before venturing back out into the larger cybersphere.

Social-emotional learning will be explored further as well in this part of the book before proceeding to recommended learning experiences. All of the different aspects of learning and development combine fairly neatly within digital civics and citizenship education. As will become evident further into the text, the instructor plays a pivotal role in navigating some of the challenging areas.

NOTES

1. Charles McCarthy, Flora Swan, and Jennie Willing McMullin, *Elementary Civics* (New York: Thompson, Brown, 1916).

2. L. D. Baker, *Civics and Citizenship: A Sourcebook for Schools* (Alberta, Canada: Regina, School Aids and Text Book Publishing Co., 1961).

3. John J. Patrick, *Lessons on the Constitution: Supplements to High School Courses in American History, Government, and Civics* (Boulder, CO: Social Science Education Consortium, 1986).

Chapter Six

Where Do We Go from Here?

How does the information presented in the chapters so far inform the state of education now and into the future? Attaining a stance similar to the Roman deity Janus, educators can both look to the past and peer into the future to realize the importance and challenge of creating an applicable digital citizenship and civics curriculum for all learning levels. The current global situation and its stark lack of a codified body of digital civics and citizenship instruction and guidance regularly reveal the necessity of this instruction.

Far too many psychological problems and emotional injuries, going so far as to result in suicide far too often, are the horrific results of poor digital citizenship and civics across populations. Yet history proves over and over again that moving forward with a nationalistic-based, authoritarian perspective, which reveals its inherent myopia, damages all involved. Thus, moving forth with an effective and accepted curriculum must be done judiciously and carefully.

Take heart—it *is* possible to navigate the novel and expanding dimension of life in the cybersphere. Adhering to the pillars of the digital civics and citizenship framework—education, respect, and advocacy—makes the challenge manageable. These three pillars can help generate a map with boundaries informed by the lessons of the past. It is important to navigate between the poles of anarchy and authoritarianism and cultivate a curriculum that not only allows for organic growth but encourages dynamic evolution.

These three pillars are a recurring theme in this book. Centuries of learning and cognitive development support these three aspects of digital civics and citizenship. These tools, even though they can be viewed as traditional, are highly useful in constructing an expanded understanding of digital existence and community, or, more fundamentally, being and belonging.

It is possible to construct a framework in which the proverbial "best of all worlds" can be examined. Then, through collaboration and compromise, individuals can collectively cultivate a respectful and informed digital existence through their actions and interactions. This provides something resembling a constantly evolving teleological and phenomenological understanding of our interactions with each other. This aspect of education informs and equips individuals to create and cultivate a digital world where direct action can have a greater impact than in the everyday, physical world. This learning experience also provides the learner with the opportunity to understand that civics and citizenship are an a priori phenomenon, existing outside of humanity and society.

Previous forays into citizenship and civics education show that it seems to allow this undercurrent to flow and bubble up within the consciousness of learners. The seemingly counterintuitive understanding that individuals have a say and choice in acting civically and being citizens can be not only revealing but also empowering if well tempered.

Perhaps the best available beacon to help guide us in achieving successful digital civics and citizenship comes from the psychoanalyst and philosopher Carl Jung. In his semiautobiographical book *Memories, Dreams, Reflections*, which was the last one published during Jung's lifetime, he states, "As far as we can discern, the sole purpose of human existence is to kindle a light in the darkness of mere being. It may even be assumed that just as the unconscious affects us, so the increase in our consciousness affects the unconscious."[1]

Of course, the focus and end goals of digital citizenship and civics education are not necessarily to answer the psychological, emotional, and spiritual questions of being and existence. However, these disciplines can provide insights that might help an individual grapple with these questions by addressing individual behaviors and actions in relation to the evolving digital world. Digital civics and citizenship are in no way tools for psychotherapy or operant conditioning, but they can be informed by these to a certain extent.

At its core, traditional citizenship and civics education is founded solidly upon an agreed-upon, if unspoken, code of behaviors and ethics. This is where teaching digital civics and citizenship requires deftness and agility. Too frequently in the past, civics and citizenship education were tantamount to indoctrination. Students would learn how to be "good and responsible citizens" without necessarily understanding why they would want to be good and responsible citizens.

So, looking to not only traditional civics and citizenship practices and methods, there are some gems among the rocks that can be shaped for use in the digital realm. The global scope of working in the digital realm requires a wide sense of awareness. Certain understandings and concepts of liberty, freedom, and democracy are colored by local hues. While foundational notions are universally true, such as the right to free speech and association and the freedom of belief and worship, perspectives in understanding vary culturally and geographically, even more so in the digital world, where borders and boundaries are seemingly nonexistent.

In a way, the digital world is something similar to the American colonies and the early national period within the history of the United States of America. An apocryphal story about Benjamin Franklin and the US Constitution helps make sense of this analogy. The story supposedly takes place in Philadelphia in 1787. Exiting what is now known as Constitutional Hall after the drafting of the Constitution, Franklin was asked by someone in the crowd if the new nation was a monarchy or a democracy. Franklin is reported to have replied, "A republic, if you can keep it."[2] So, we must work and struggle to maintain the digital republic that the internet has helped to make possible.

The digital realm is far removed physically and chronologically from the American colonies and the early United States. Yet some crucial pieces of culture and understanding can be extracted from both. The concepts and practices of respect, advocacy, and education are almost universally acknowledged. These three pillars allow construction of the proverbial hall.

In traditional civics and citizenship education, many of the practices and understandings taught are solidly based in sociological concepts and the actions of community groups. Consider freedom of speech as an example. While even in the United States the understanding of what constitutes free speech continues to be debated, the core concept is founded upon respect and advocacy. It entails an individual having a voice and the inalienable right to speak and share with others. In turn, other individuals constituting the local community have a responsibility to allow individuals to express their understandings and points of view.

On the other hand, the community also has the responsibility to ensure that what individuals say does not necessarily cause panic or harm. Likewise, individuals must consider their words and messages in terms of the expected outcomes of sharing them. This is found at the root of Jean-Jacques Rousseau's theory of freedom as set forth in his foundational work, *The Social Contract*. Ensuring freedom, in this sense the freedom of expression, is more solidly based upon disagreeing with the message or its means of communication but still providing an arena for its expression.

A quote from the same time period provides a sentiment that helps to concisely sum up this precarious balance between freedom and responsibility. Voltaire is often credited as having said, "I disapprove of what you say, but I will defend to the death your right to say it."[3] The actual quote, its exact wording, and even its context continue to be debated among historical, philosophical, and even linguistic scholars. However, the sentiment expressed is the heart of not only a democratic society, but also of civics and citizenship education.

In a certain sense, whereas traditional civics and citizenship education taught students fervent national pride, digital civics and citizenship requires something very different and yet perhaps even stronger: resilience. One of the key facets of social-emotional learning is resilience. Perhaps this is what can be taught in the place of nationalism. Doing so might not only allow individuals to express their opinions but also allow others to express theirs. Resiliency, in this sense, is a type of inner strength possessed by an individual. This strength serves as the foundation for the confidence needed to express an opinion and to be faced with disagreement that can be ugly at times.

With this understanding, digital civics and citizenship education is just as much character education as it is teaching a traditional content area. Students can learn ideas and actions pertaining to digital civics and citizenship without being anchored to a particular nationality or political persuasion. Similarly, digital civics and citizenship takes on the flavor or hue of vocational education. Being a digital citizen is a vocation.

We all have the opportunity, as do future generations, to create a virtual, Western-style democracy within the digital realm. At the same time, the opportunity exists for something oppressive and totalitarian to come into being in the virtual world. Perhaps more so than at any other time in human history, each individual has as close to an equal voice and responsibility as ever witnessed to determine which type of virtual existence will be created and experienced. Each person has access to the tools that can either build up or tear down the value of the digital realm.

NOTES

1. Carl G. Jung, *Memories, Dreams, Reflections*, ed. Aniela Jaffé (Waukegan, IL: Fontana Press, 1972).
2. https://constitutioncenter.org/learn/educational-resources/historical-documents/perspectives-on-the-constitution-a-republic-if-you-can-keep-it.
3. Evelyn Beatrice Hall, *The Friends of Voltaire* (London: Putnam, 1906).

Chapter Seven

Social-Emotional Learning and Cultural Literacy

Along with an exploration of social-emotional learning and cultural literacy, this chapter provides an opportunity to identify how these two pedagogies within education complement each other when taught through digital civics and citizenship instruction and practice. Social-emotional learning is a topic that grabs headlines not only in various education industry journals and trade publications but also in the mainstream media. This is due in large part to the increased usage of digital media by students at an increasingly early age. Digital technology has become ubiquitous in people's daily lives, including in education.

The marked impact that digital technology, specifically social media, has on individuals is daily becoming more evident. The rise of cyberbullying, as well as digital crimes throughout the world, reveals the need for social-emotional learning within digital civics and citizenship education. End users of digital technology need a civic framework informed by a foundational ethical understanding in order to interact with others digitally.

Social-emotional learning provides individuals with the tools and understanding necessary for considering others as well as for protecting themselves within the digital sphere.

Likewise, the mostly forgotten arena of cultural literacy[1] that came to prominence in the 1980s remains a significant factor in education regardless of the context. However, the expanding digital realm somewhat revives its importance. This particular focus on identifying, understanding, appreciating, and transmitting shared cultural practices, knowledge, and mores from one generation to the next is a foundational aspect of education as a whole. In many nations, particularly the United States of America, the multicultural nature of the citizenry challenges the nation as a whole to continually redefine, to a certain extent, what it means to be an American, and just exactly what is America in a shared, cultural understanding.

SOCIAL-EMOTIONAL LEARNING

Social-emotional learning has been a facet of education, particularly K–12 education, for decades. This arises in the curriculum regularly throughout the history of public education, just under a different moniker each time. Social-emotional learning and character development courses have been known as etiquette, civics education, citizenship lessons, and even simply manners.

However, social-emotional learning has made something of a comeback in recent years, primarily due to the increased exposure to and use of social media by younger individuals. The impact of this is readily evident throughout numerous reports published in the mainstream media, along with peer-reviewed industry journals. Evidence of this impact includes mental health issues, socialization challenges, and even, sadly enough, adolescent and teenage suicide. Some portions of society have attached labels to this phenomenon such as "epidemic" and "menace." Regardless of the name, the fact that social media and ostensibly digital technology is a significant contribution to the phenomenon is evident.

To effectively employ current and traditional methods of social-emotional learning, it is important to understand what it is. The Collaborative for Academic, Social, Emotional Learning (CASEL) defines social-emotional learning this way:

> Social and emotional learning (SEL) is the process through which children and adults understand and manage emotions, set and achieve positive goals, feel and show empathy for others, establish and maintain positive relationships, and make responsible decisions.[2]

This definition and understanding serves as part of the foundation upon which the recommended methods for digital civics and citizenship education in this text are built. Examining the history of SEL helps gain a deeper understanding.

Looking at the offerings that were available in the past, especially in K–12 public education, shows the bits and pieces of the more concentrated whole that is now available for students to experience through social-emotional education. Students received lessons on manners, behavior, and civic acts as part of their development. They were instructed on behaviors not only in the classroom, but within the larger context of the school building and campus. Certain actions and behaviors were expected even outside of the boundaries of the school, such as at crosswalks as students walked to and from school daily. Given the fact that school campuses and districts supplied the crossing guards—traditionally, older students from the local campus—a certain amount of responsibility training and peer mentoring occurred.

In traditional settings, whether K–12 or higher education, students were exposed to moral and civic training through courses in Latin. Regardless of whether students suffered through, barely survived, or even succeeded in these classes, they were exposed to the writings of Marcus Aurelius, Seneca, Zeno, Epictetus, and others. These thinkers are most closely associated with the philosophy and practice of Stoicism. Embedded within this philosophy, or code of conduct, is individual and civic responsibility, among other qualities and virtues.

Students often translated selected written pieces from these authors. Through this translation work, they explored ideas such as personal responsibility, civic responsibility, respect, civic virtue, and social actions. This learning experience is crucial in seeing not only what can be learned from the past, but also how it can inform digital civics and citizenship education.

Translation is challenging. It is not the mere act of finding the word equivalent in the translator's language to match what the writer has written. Rather, it requires the individual working with a foreign text to embody the writer, as best as can be done, in the particular context in which the piece was composed. The hermeneutics of translation demands that the translator communicate the message as authentically as possible as intended by the author. Translating is not transcribing; rather, it is sharing the message in the way in which it was originally intended.

In these classes, students working with ancient texts were challenged to consider not just what had been written but why it was written. Answering the question of why these topics were important enough to record for posterity is one of the hinges of translating. Understanding the intended impact the writer expected plays a crucial role in translating effectively. Through translating, students studied some of the foundational thinkers of civics and citizenship who have informed and who influence current thinking.

While the act of translating itself will not necessarily communicate the desired attitudes, behaviors, and actions that digital civics and citizenship hopes to convey to learners, it at least provides students with exposure to these things that they may not have encountered before. Traits such as respect, civility, civic-mindedness, and other similar attitudes and behaviors are ensconced in many of the classical writings of Greece, Rome, China, and India. Similarly, they form the basis of classical Western liberal thought, which in turn influenced the foundations of modern democratic governments.

Through the act of translation, discussions regarding the nature of courage, respect, individual and shared responsibility, and other civic traits is inevitable. Through the course of translating not merely for technical accuracy but also for nuance of mood, subtext, and context, a discussion of what the traits embody naturally arises. Added to this, the conversation between instructor and learner can naturally evolve into what these particular traits look like in practice in a variety of settings and how they influence local culture as well as national character. In other words, one of the primary goals of translation exercises from a digital civics and citizenship perspective is as a bridge to opening discussions with a certain latitude provided for analysis.

The resurgence of Stoicism and Stoic philosophy has some cultural critics and pundits dismissing it as a fad that will soon fade back into history. However, its impact on the current practice and perspective of civics and citizenship can inform the practices of these things within the cybersphere. While this may seem counterintuitive, using technology as a pathway to exploring classical philosophy actually makes sense. Apart from digital civics and citizenship, discussions about such things as the nature of reality, psychological and sociological constructs, and the evolution of character can spring up.

By providing exposure to these ideas and their originators through digital civics and citizenship, to include traditional exercises in translation, learners have something like a double exposure. First, learners have the opportunity to encounter these great thinkers, as well as others, through their works in their original languages. In this way, a learner must grapple with the ideas in their original format, translating them for themselves and not relying on another's efforts. Second, learners are provided the opportunity to investigate and practice the actions and character traits espoused in these classical works in a contemporary digital setting. In doing so, learners have the opportunity to experiment and modify these traits in order to best fit them into their own unique contexts.

Ironically, it is in the digital sphere that the need for strong personal bearings with regard to behavior and decision making, or civics and citizenship, is most strongly felt. Consider the extensive coverage in the mainstream media of cyberbullying, which too often ends with the target committing suicide. To address this issue, educators and mental health professionals are focusing their efforts in social-emotional learning on building resiliency within the younger generations.

This is necessary for the overall health and well-being of our global society and culture. However, resiliency is not a cure-all or a silver bullet. It is a vital component to responding to this challenge, but it is not the only answer. Resiliency requires that all parties involved take responsibility for their actions. More is needed to overcome this challenging and complex situation. In fact, digital civics and citizenship education is another vital part of the solution. Like resiliency, digital civics and citizenship is part and parcel of social-emotional learning.

Digital civics and citizenship draw on knowledge and skills from a myriad of content areas, including STEM and the humanities. In these learning domains, students are challenged not only to share their ideas and perspectives but to support them as objectively as possible. In the same manner, students are challenged to listen and consider other points of view. As explored earlier, classical philosophy and current technology also play roles in the mixture of influences on digital civics and citizenship.

While digital civics and citizenship education and practice is not a cure-all, it does allow for deeper and more complex conversations about moral actions and philosophy within public life. This is the foundation of social-emotional learning. Learning resiliency together with appropriate civic acts and positive citizenship equips learners with the tools and behaviors needed to not only protect themselves but to also positively engage with others, both in person and in the digital realm.

CULTURAL LITERACY

In the 1980s, a small but lasting idea in public education quickly grew into a fairly significant movement whose legacy endures in the background today. E. D. Hirsch coined the term *cultural literacy* and made it a popular educational buzzword with the publication of *Cultural Literacy* in 1988. Many educators and policy makers embraced the theory and practice posited by Hirsch in his seminal work to the point that Hirsch and others established the Core Knowledge Foundation just a year before the publication of the book.

Hirsch framed his theory of cultural literacy based on his own experience as a college professor and classroom experiments with his students. His initial perspective was founded upon the students' understanding, or lack thereof, with regard to being a citizen of the United States and the rights and responsibilities that apply.

Thomas Jefferson said that he would prefer newspapers without government to government without newspapers. He thought that the very concept of American democracy, depending as it does on all citizens having a vote, requires an informed citizenry and universal literacy. He thought that literate, well-informed citizens would be able, more often than not, to make decisions in their collective best interest. On Jefferson's principles, we might venture this definition of the background information that an American citizen ought to have in order to be truly literate: it is the background information required to read serious American newspapers and magazines with understanding. This knowledge would include not only political, proverbial, and historical information but also scientific information as part of the general background knowledge that I am calling "cultural literacy."[3]

Like the earlier examinations of *civitas* and *eudaimonia*, Hirsch's initial identification of cultural literacy is based upon a traditional understanding of society, culture, and citizenship. However, he expanded this point of view to include that cultural literacy also informs and influences individuals' daily lives and interactions with one another. There is enough truth in the idea that literacy is a set of transferable skills to make such educational formalism a respectable, if inadequate, theory to hold. But it should be added that in recent times this skills-based approach has also been a safe theory to hold. Specialists in reading and writing who adopt the skills-based approach needn't commit themselves to any particular content or values, except the values of so-called "pluralism." They can present themselves as technicians who remain above the cultural battle. This posture of neutral expertness is nowhere better illustrated than in the official curriculum guides of certain states (for instance, the state of California), which mention no specific content at all. In earlier days, American educators carefully combined the technical skills of reading and writing with background knowledge, that is to say, with the acculturative side of literacy teaching. But in our own day, after fifty years of the skills-based approach, and despite the advances we have made in reading research and in educating the disadvantaged, we find a decline in SAT scores and an apparent increase in cultural fragmentation.[4]

Even though Hirsch was writing about the decline in public awareness of the history and government of the United States, at least at the federal level, in the book, the point of view was expanded to include a more holistic understanding of certain facets of culture such as literature and the arts. In an article published in 2009, the impetus of Hirsch's research and theory were laid out to explain the connection between his past academic work and his shift to cultural literacy.

This finding, first published in a psychology journal, was consistent with Hirsch's past scholarship, in which he had argued that the author takes for granted that his readers have crucial background knowledge. Hirsch was also convinced that the problem of inadequate background knowledge began in the early grades. Elementary school teachers thus had to be more explicit about imparting such knowledge to students—indeed, this was even more important than teaching the "skills" of reading and writing, Hirsch believed. Hirsch's insight contravened the conventional wisdom in the nation's schools: that teaching facts was unimportant and that students instead should learn "how-to" skills.[5]

The fact that this excerpt is from over a decade ago and that it's based on findings and analysis from the 1980s is often used to refute or overlook the suggestions Hirsch made. Yet we see some of the same things that Hirsch said were the impetus for his research compounded in our current time. Evidence exists in the many media pieces where a personality or reporter stops random individuals on the street and asks them questions about US history, the government, and current events. The results are typically the same: complete lack of a working knowledge in these areas in most random samplings of individuals.

Similarly, the rise of outcome-based education, especially in the secondary and tertiary levels of instruction, continues to dominate policy and funding discussions in education. In high schools, colleges, and universities, faculty and administrators are scrutinizing their work due to the increased, if inadvertent, pressure students are placing on these institutions regarding courses they enroll in and degree programs they pursue.

In other words, educational administrators and policy makers are following the money. Most often, the money (e.g., tuition payments) flows in the direction of degrees and programs that promise, and most often deliver, job opportunities upon completion or graduation. This is not a far-fetched idea to understand. Given the cost of attending a college or university, students, being savvy consumers, want to make sure they get a return on their investment. However, focusing so much on outcomes, particularly professional outcomes, may encroach on these educational bodies and organizations in truly educating their students rather than merely training them.

Cultural literacy dovetails nicely with digital civics and citizenship and with social-emotional learning in that all three approaches to learning and their curricula seek to teach and practice shared behaviors among individuals within a community in order that the community may be open, equitable, and respectful for all its constituent members. In many ways, these different pedagogies overlap in crucial areas. Perhaps the best way of understanding these three different educational pedagogies is through the lens of language.

Students are shown that words have a variety of meanings, and those meanings can be shaded by their use. Similarly, learners find out that the English language has a specific and defined, yet flexible, framework of use, or mechanics and syntax, as it is formally known. Lastly, learners come to understand and appreciate that language is used differently in different contexts. This understanding provides a greater level of success and competency in users when communicating with a variety of audiences in a diversity of settings.

Carrying this metaphor of understanding further, social-emotional learning provides a framework of understanding and appreciating the variety of meanings certain behaviors, attitudes, and actions have. Digital civics and citizenship supplies the interactive framework. Cultural literacy is the interchangeable lens individuals can employ to successfully and respectfully interact in a variety of contexts. In other words, these three pedagogies provide an applied lens not just to understanding the content, but to successfully applying it in everyday life. The expectation is that by learning and practicing, individuals will cultivate a deep and dynamic respect for these pedagogies, informed by classical philosophy, in regard to interacting with others, especially in a digital context.

The combination of social-emotional learning, cultural literacy, and digital civics and citizenship may seem antithetical to the current state of education. However, digital civics and citizenship, informed by social-emotional learning and cultural literacy, may be an important and vital step in bridging the traditional notion of education and the trend of outcome-based learning that is currently guiding K–12 and higher education. As will be explored in greater depth later in this text, digital civics and citizenship may provide an amalgamation of traditional educational content and current digital technology.

SYNTHESIS

Taking a step back from these dives into social-emotional learning and cultural literacy, the primary question of their impact on digital civics and citizenship still needs to be answered. Part of the answer will be evident in the next section of the text as recommended learning experiences and recommended approaches are provided. However, these do not completely answer the question.

Incorporating a larger, less academic perspective, the roles that social-emotional learning and cultural literacy play in digital civics and citizenship become apparent for learners and educators. To successfully function and engage others within the digital sphere, individuals need to have not only resiliency but also a certain depth of empathy and awareness toward others and their context. This functional depth of awareness is arrived at in part by cultural literacy.

Expanding from the understanding that Hirsch's research and writing has provided, *digital* cultural literacy moves into the nebulous area of the digital sphere. Helping individuals understand and appreciate (e.g., become "literate" in) their own culture serves as a basis as well as a tool for attaining a level of emerging literacy in the cultures of those with whom they engage online. In other words, embodying literacy in one's culture serves as the starting point for becoming literate in another culture. To use a business term, this cultural literacy effort is scalable.

Paralleling this sense of cultural "awareness" is social-emotional learning. Almost replicating the incorporation of cultural literacy into digital civics and citizenship, an individual with a functional level of self-awareness and self-understanding can find encountering and engaging with new and seemingly foreign individuals somewhat easier. While this is not a guaranteed solution for creating a digitally civil world, it will facilitate more respectful communication and exchanges between individuals in different communities and cultures.

Incorporating these two bodies of knowledge and their attendant practices provides educators and learners with tools and understandings to smooth out some of the friction points that arise from interpersonal communication, especially within the digital realm. Social-emotional learning and cultural literacy play important roles as facets of digital civics and citizenship instruction. As individuals become more active in the digital sphere, the skills of communication and collaboration with a diverse population grow more significant for anyone to successfully navigate society in all its myriad contexts.

NOTES

1. E. D. Hirsch, *Cultural Literacy: What Every American Needs to Know* (New York: Vintage, 1988).

2. https://casel.org/what-is-sel.

3. E. D. Hirsch, Jr., "Cultural Literacy" (paper presented at the National Adult Literacy Conference, Washington, DC, January 19–20, 1984).

4. Ibid.

5. Sol Stern, "E. D. Hirsch's Curriculum for Democracy," *City Journal*, Manhattan Institute for Policy, Autumn 2009.

Chapter Eight

Virtue Ethics and Digital Civics and Citizenship

The ideas and philosophies of some of Western civilization's greatest minds, such as Plato and Aristotle, have been discussed in relation to digital civics and citizenship. While many millennia separate the current world from theirs, the ancient understanding and perspective on living an ethical and moral life in terms of individual and civic development have quite a lot to share with the current social situation, especially in a digital sense.

Among these classical philosophers and within this subset of thought, an idea coalesced around the ethical ideals of a "good life" and "civic responsibility." This text has explored the concept of *eudaimonia*—flourishing—but the idea of the "good life" needs some attention. It comes from a combination of the Greek words *arete* and *phronesis*.

Arete can be roughly translated into English as meaning "excellence" or "virtue." As with almost any word taken from the ancient language, *arete* has a variety of meanings depending on its usage. However, in the context of this discussion, *arete* can be understood as a kind of excellence that an individual has attained through effort. More specifically, it describes a type of moral excellence or virtue exhibited by an individual.

History reveals to even the casual scholar that these ideas and ideals, along with many others, from Ancient Greece, influenced the foundations of modern democracy and civil society in the West. As such, understanding and appreciating them is crucial in adapting these traits and behaviors for use in digital civics and citizenship. One of the more traditional, yet still effective, ways of exploring these traits is to expose learners to them through reading classical literature. This learning experience was explored in the previous chapter in more depth.

There is one current understanding of the good life that many of these philosophers would balk at: *arete* had nothing to do with worldly riches or luxury. Instead, it was solidly founded upon moral actions, courage, and a certain amount of humility for leavening. Heroic examples of *arete* can be found in Penelope and Odysseus, who play central roles in the *Odyssey*.

In the Hellenic world, it was believed that moral and virtuous individuals may be rewarded monetarily, but that was more a result of their temperance and moderation in spending and acquiring than being a marker of living the good life. This paradigm shift happened later and persists into our current era.

Virtue ethics can be understood as not only a philosophy of living a good and moral life but a set of ethical actions as well. Aristotle codified these actions and provided examples of what they would look like in his foundational work, *Nicomachean Ethics*.[1] According to Aristotle, there are eleven virtues that all individuals should strive to embody:

1. courage
2. temperance
3. liberality
4. magnificence
5. magnanimity
6. proper ambition
7. truthfulness
8. wittiness
9. friendliness
10. modesty
11. righteous indignation

Before Aristotle enumerated and explained these eleven virtues, Plato explored what came to be known as the four cardinal virtues. These are wisdom, justice, fortitude, and temperance. Plato examined these in his foundational work, *The Republic*.[2] This influenced subsequent thinkers and writers from Aristotle through current philosophers.

Aristotle and later moral philosophers have provided ever-evolving definitions and analyses of these virtues as they apply to living a good life. Virtue philosophy was revived, to a certain extent, as a serious field of philosophical study beginning in the Enlightenment and the Scientific Revolution. Many historians identify this renewed interest partially as resulting from the rise of Theism and atheism in Western Europe at the time. Philosophers and others were searching for a body of knowledge or a school of thought that could guide people in living a moral life without the idea of traditional religion in the Judeo-Christian understanding.

Notable philosophers such as Immanuel Kant, David Hume, and even Niccolò Machiavelli revisited the writings and teachings of Socrates and Aristotle, the later Roman philosophers Livy and Cicero, and the moral historians Plutarch and Tacitus. Even drawing upon the Judeo-Christian analyses of St. Ambrose of Milan and St. Thomas Aquinas helps to inform the postmodern and post-Christian/religious world that we currently live in, as is evident in Hume's and Kant's writings.[3]

The founders of the United States were deeply influenced by the precepts of virtue ethics and moral philosophy. This was due to not only the ways in which these men were educated but also their aspirations and hopes for the fledgling nation they were trying to form. The influence of virtue ethics and moral philosophy is evident in the foundational documents of the United States, the Declaration of Independence and the Constitution, including the Bill of Rights.

Virtue ethics were understood as a tool—a very important tool. In some ways, virtue ethics are akin to a multitool. They help to guide and govern not only civil society but also the actions of each person in that society. Unlike laws, regulations, and ordinances, virtue ethics are derived in equal parts from intrinsic and extrinsic motivators. Furthermore, virtue ethics provide society with something like an ad hoc agreement as to the "glue" that binds a group together socially and helps individuals cohere into a group through a shared body of behaviors, beliefs, and expectations.

The adhesive that is provided by virtue ethics is something that must be taught and exhibited. More importantly, virtue ethics are universal across a civilization. This immutable fact is crucial to appreciating the power that resided in virtue ethics. Psychologist Jordan B. Peterson speaks about this fact of civil society in his address delivered at the Oxford Union.

> One of the consequences is that it's tribal, and tribal identities tend towards mayhem. Now the alternative low resolution view is the view that I think has been articulated most effectively in the West, and perhaps of all the places where it's been most effectively articulated in the West, the most effective articulation has come from the U.K. There's something remarkable about what your country has done with regards to laying out the idea of individual sovereignty in a fully articulated manner, in a way that allows a political system to arise predicated on the assumption that the individual is of intrinsic value. If you need a thumbnail view of the world, the most effective thumbnail view of the world isn't that you are the member of a tribe—even though in many ways you are, and a member of many tribes. The most effective thumbnail view is that you are going to be regarded as a sovereign individual, and you are to treat other people that way as well. Both with regards to their rights, but even more importantly and often forgotten, with regards to their responsibilities.[4]

What Peterson is suggesting is contentious in some circles based upon a misinterpretation that he is advocating a "forced" responsibility on individuals. However, taking a different, perhaps less emotional point of view about this quote, an interesting dichotomy arises. From a social and civil point of view, this issue can be anchored to the dilemma of free speech in a liberal and democratic society. Peterson addresses this seemingly tricky problem in his third lecture from his "Maps of Meaning" series.

> I regard free speech as a prerequisite to a civilized society, because freedom of speech means that you can have combat with words. That's what it means. It doesn't mean that people can happily and gently exchange opinions. It means that we can engage in combat with words, in the battleground of ideas. And the reason that that's acceptable, and why it's acceptable that people's feelings get hurt during that combat, is that the combat of ideas is far preferable to actual combat.[5]

Yet this dilemma reaches further within the individual psyches of the people who populate a particular social group, society, or civilization. In the same lecture, Peterson shows how the biblical story of Cain and Abel informs a modern understanding of many of the social struggles found in our current civilization.

> The kids are starting to burn this place and to trash it. They're dragging a grand piano down the stairs. It's the destruction of high culture, about which they're nothing but cynical, because they don't believe that hard work and sacrifice can produce something of any value. They want to bring it down and destroy it. You can see it in the story of Cain and Abel. Abel is hard working, and everyone likes him, and he makes the proper sacrifices, so his life goes really well. And that's part of the reason that Cain hates him. He's jealous and resentful, but worse than that—if you're not doing very well and you're around someone who is doing very well it's painful, because the mere fact of their Being judges you. And so it's very easy to want to destroy that ideal so that you don't have to live with the terrible consequences of seeing it embodied in front of you. And so part of the reason that people want to tear things down is so that they don't have anything to contrast themselves against and to feel bad. And that's exactly what's happening here.
>
> Kids are destroying all of this culture, because the fact that it exists judges them.[6]

Along with this viewpoint, take in the growing amount of scientific evidence about the negative impact that prolonged and regular exposure to and use of social media has on individuals, especially individuals who are still developing socially, cognitively, and physically.[7] The need becomes evident to revive, reinvigorate, and renovate citizenship and civics education, focusing on the digital realm.

While approaching the challenge of teaching these traits to learners in all contexts, the obstacle of recognizing boundaries between individuals as well as between the state and the citizen is crucial. As educators, it is incumbent upon us to provide options to learners in order to honor individual choice and freedom. However, in exploring these civil traits and virtues, learners need to be provided the opportunity to "try on" these different behaviors and attitudes experientially through preferred actions within the learning environment.

Yet this regular act of lining up orderly offers to learners a tremendous experience in exploring and practicing the same civil behaviors that are needed in a digital environment. It is common that most individuals want to be either first in line or as close to first as possible. Yet virtue ethics dictates that we balance our wants with the needs of the entire group. In this particular case, students can learn that accepting their place in line is just as noble as achieving the first place in line.

Similarly, when interacting with others online, individuals who have learned not simply the *how* of lining up in person orderly but also the *why* of this act can converse online with a variety of individuals in a civil and respectful way. As one learns to line up orderly in a physical environment, they can also apply these behaviors and actions to discussing a topic with others online. When a topic is being discussed or even debated online, an individual can practice accepting their place in the group, patiently awaiting their turn and respecting the place and time of others in the group.

In learning and practicing digital civics and citizenship, individuals come to understand and appreciate that respectful disagreement is a common exchange in a liberal democracy and civil society. Likewise, individuals learn that allowing each individual their appropriate time and place is crucial for an equitable exchange. Perhaps the greatest "lesson" learned from lining up orderly in person that is immediately transferrable to an online environment is that exchanges and discussions are not always a contest. All individuals involved will end up where they originally intended to be. Whether they were at the head of the line, in the middle, or at the end, the destination does not change. As such, asserting and attaining dominance in these discussions is actually antithetical to their very nature.

Individually, these traits and actions when carried over into digital civics and citizenship turn the focus inward. When a respectful disagreement occurs between two individuals or within a group, it is incumbent upon all involved to reflect on their own actions and beliefs. In other words, we are all called upon to check ourselves and where we are. In doing so, we accept the possibility that we may be the one in the wrong. In his latest book, *12 Rules for Life: An Antidote to Chaos*, Dr. Jordan Peterson extolled the virtue of self-reflection and improvement in his sixth rule. In this rule, Peterson admonishes readers, "If you can't even clean up your own room, who the hell are you to give advice to the world? My sense is that if you want to change the world, you start with yourself and work outward because you build your competence that way."[8] Learning and practicing virtue ethics and civic virtues in person, through a learning experience, equips individuals for encountering others in the digital sphere with respect, not only for the others they encounter but also for themselves.

Moving citizenship and civics education into the digital realm, educators are faced with a novel challenge. As Peterson shares in the second quote above, the innate desire for a person to compare themselves with someone who appears to be wildly successful on social media is not only dangerous but debilitating. Digital civics and citizenship could shoulder part of the responsibility for expanding individuals' digital literacy to understand the fact that what they are seeing is either that individual at their best or is entirely staged and thus fake.

Returning to the first quote from Peterson, digital civics and citizenship educators must also guard against indoctrinating students into what can be thought of as a political theology. Traditionally, civics and citizenship education often lapsed into this realm. As a result, this facet of education was perceived as indoctrination and training rather than education and learning. A heightened awareness of this shadowy part of the legacy of civics and citizenship education is crucial to not merely avoid repeating past mistakes but also to cultivate evolution, adaptation, and ultimately adoption in the digital realm.

One way to help increase demand for digital civics and citizenship education is by leveraging the current resurgence in the popularity of Stoicism. This philosophy from Ancient Greece, further cultivated in classical Rome, provides a bona fide path for educators. Recently, Stoicism has experienced resurgence, especially among young digital professionals. Many in the Silicon Valley workforce have adopted this philosophical stance on life in the quest to achieve a "good life" in an ethical way without adhering to any particular religious tradition.

While the worthiness of this application is a discussion for another time, Stoicism does have an impact on digital civics and citizenship. That impact is worth examining, and the influence is a positive one. Stoicism is a demanding philosophy that was popular among slaves and workers in Ancient Greece. In fact, its name comes from the Greek term *stoa*, which means "entryway," or what would be called a porch today. This was due to the fact that slaves and lower-class workmen were not allowed in gymnasia where philosophical, political, and other such conversations were carried on.

Stoicism was originally something of an antidote to the harsh external realities that slaves and lower-class workmen had to endure. Under the Romans, it blossomed into an internal philosophy of controlling one's reactions to events that are beyond one's control. Stoicism was celebrated by the emperor Marcus Aurelius, who added to the body of knowledge. He also added prestige and renown to the philosophy, making it more palatable and even praiseworthy in many parts of Roman society. In fact, many of his quotes are still popular today, such as this one: "The tranquility that comes when you stop caring what they say. Or think, or do. Only what you do."[9]

For the purposes of digital civics and citizenship, Stoicism provides many useful tools for preparing individuals to practice respect and advocacy in an online environment. Many of the teachings of Stoicism challenge practitioners and adherents to control their emotions and work on what they can control themselves, rather than feeding the frustration of trying to control the situation, which is usually not possible. Another Roman, Seneca, addressed this lifelong challenge with the admonition, "It does not matter what you bear, but how you bear it."[10]

Teaching and practicing this may help individuals to control their emotional reactions, which heavily populate social media and mainstream media today. It can also provide tools for people to defend themselves from cyberbullying attacks and help to mitigate such situations. Individuals can also learn to provide advocacy for others who may experience cyberbullying, trolling, or other such attacks that are all too frequent events on social media.

Stoicism in this manner provides an entry point for individuals to practice advocacy within the cybersphere. Like other recommendations and methods examined in this text, Stoicism is neither a cure-all nor a magic pill that will right all wrongs and reverse course on bullying and other social ills exhibited online.

Yet Stoicism does provide individuals with the necessary tools for navigating online communities, as well as physical communities, in their lives. Given the basis of respect and fortitude that Stoicism espouses, an individual practicing Stoic philosophy in their attitude and behavior can not only speak to other individuals with some authority about respecting others but advocate for them as well. The courage needed to verbalize self-advocacy is a firm foundation upon which to expand advocating for others.

Verbal advocacy is part and parcel of the recognized right to free speech. English political philosopher John Stuart Mill based the thesis of his seminal work, *On Liberty*, on this very right. He also recognized the balance between individual liberties and social responsibilities in regard to freedom of speech. The following excerpt illustrates Mill's indefatigable perspective that informs and influences this approach to digital civics and citizenship.

> Protection, therefore, against the tyranny of the magistrate is not enough: there needs protection also against the tyranny of the prevailing opinion and feeling; against the tendency of society to impose, by other means than civil penalties, its own ideas and practices as rules of conduct on those who dissent from them; to fetter the development, and, if possible, prevent the formation, of any

individuality not in harmony with its ways, and compel all characters to fashion themselves upon the model of its own. There is a limit to the legitimate
interference of collective opinion with individual independence: and to find
that limit, and maintain it against encroachment, is as indispensable to a good
condition of human affairs, as protection against political despotism.[11]

Mill provides us with the enduring understanding that freedom of speech
is not only an enduring right, but the responsibility of each and every citizen
in a democratic society. Now this includes the digital realm. Without appearing to be nationalistic or even jingoistic, individuals can respect, advocate
for, and educate each other about treating others with the inherent dignity
each human being is endowed with through their being.

With this combination of Stoicism and virtue ethics in mind, entering into
the education and practice of digital civics and citizenship takes on a new
depth and complexity. Caution, awareness, and respect should guide individuals' movements into and within the cybersphere to both enjoy a positive
experience and cultivate positive experiences with others. Interaction in the
digital realm requires many of the same understandings, mores, and rules that
interpersonal interactions demand in a physical setting.

NOTES

1. J. E. C. Welldon, trans. and ed., *The Nicomachean Ethics of Aristotle, with Critical Analysis* (London: Macmillan, 1897).

2. I. A. Richards, trans. and ed., *Plato's Republic* (Cambridge: Cambridge University Press, 1966).

3. William Durant, *The Story of Philosophy* (New York: Simon & Schuster, 1926).

4. https://www.jordanbpeterson.com/transcripts/oxford-union.

5. Jordan Peterson, "Marionettes and Individuals," Maps of Meaning Lecture Series 4 (2017).

6. Peterson, "Marionettes and Individuals."

7. Gwenn Schurgin O'Keeffe and Kathleen Clarke-Pearson, "The Impact of Social Media on Children, Adolescents, and Families," *Council on Communications and Media Pediatrics* 127, no. 4 (April 2011): 800–804, https://doi.org/10.1542/peds.2011-0054.

8. Jordan B. Peterson, *12 Rules for Life: An Antidote to Chaos* (New York: Random House, 2018).

9. D. Estes, *The Thoughts of Marcus Aurelius Antoninus* (Oxford: Oxford University Press, 1980).

10. Lucius Annaeus Seneca, *The Stoic Philosophy of Seneca: Essays and Letters of Seneca* (London: Norton, 1968).

11. John Stuart Mill, *On Liberty* (London: Parker, 1959).

Part Two

Examples

Chapter Nine

Approach to Teaching Digital Civics and Citizenship

In any learning situation, it is the teacher who establishes the feel, the environment, and the tone of the experience at the beginning. Like the director of a stage play or a film, the teacher sets the entire mood of the experience, both consciously and unconsciously. While this may not seem like a major issue when teaching and learning digital civics and citizenship, it actually is a significant factor in this and in all learning experiences.

In fact, it is through the teacher's speech, actions, and behaviors that students can sometimes learn the most enduring lessons. The role of the teacher includes advocacy, resilience, humility, curiosity, and other aspects. Consider the following examples.

In an elementary school classroom, most often the teacher's tone of voice, word choice, actions, and behaviors are gentle and encouraging. This is crucial to foster a love of learning and cultivate the innate curiosity of the students. This blends well with the natural curiosity that most younger students embody. However, at the secondary level, there is a noticeable shift in the teacher's tone of voice, word choice, actions, and behaviors. Of course, the most obvious difference is in the linguistic register. The vocabulary is more advanced compared to elementary school, as well it should be. However, the tone is also more mature, at a time when many students are grappling with adult realities outside of school.

In digital civics and citizenship education, the impact of the teacher's delivery is crucial for learners. Teachers are learning leaders. Just as a leader in any organization sets the tone for the working environment, so too does a teacher set the tone for the learning environment. In other words, if a teacher does not see the value in what they are teaching, the students won't value the knowledge and skills being taught.

TEACHER BUY-IN

Given the understanding of the subject matter that has been laid out, it is evident that the first group that must understand the importance of teaching and learning digital civics and citizenship is teachers. The faculty need to believe in what they are teaching. Now, this belief does not need to be a slavish devotion or blind adherence. Rather, it must be a level of trust that teachers recognize and understand the value of what is being taught in their classroom. Just as the core areas of language arts, social studies, science, and mathematics are understood as essential for students to be successful not only in school but also in life, digital civics and citizenship are just as vital.

Most individuals who enter into the vocation of teaching have an innate desire to help others and see them succeed. This is a powerful place to start to cultivate teacher buy-in for teaching digital civics and citizenship, since learning this topic prepares students to successfully navigate, communicate in, and contribute to our growing global society. It provides students with the understanding and skills needed to be safe and successful in the digital sphere.

One example of this is internet safety. Often, children and adolescents share personal information with other individuals online, believing these people to be friends or at least sympathetic listeners. Sadly, this can lead to abuse, exploitation, and in some extreme cases even abduction or death for the child or adolescent. Think of it this way: there is no teacher practicing today who would object to students learning safe ways of crossing a street or interacting with strangers. The fact is that these skills have migrated into the digital sphere.

Digital civics and citizenship prepare students with the knowledge and skills needed for our world.

PROFESSIONAL DEVELOPMENT

It is not uncommon in most traditional educational settings that professional development is required with the adoption of a new curriculum or a new instructional program. For digital civics and citizenship, it is no different. More so than in most educational professional development, the recommended training and preparation for digital civics and citizenship instructors contains an essential participatory piece that extends well beyond formal training.

In most cases, professional development for educators is anywhere from a half day to a few days spent with a trainer or other representative from the vendor supplying the materials that will be used for instruction. This time is spent familiarizing educators with all the facets of the program or curriculum, especially highlighting what makes the program different from or more successful than the competition. In a sense, a certain portion of the training is devoted to building comfort, confidence, and support for the product itself.

The recommended professional development for digital civics and citizenship educators at any level, and for any participant population, can be roughly divided into three phases. The following is a brief survey of those phases.

Phase 1

The first phase of recommended professional development for teachers of digital civics and citizenship education is fairly similar to any other traditional professional development for educators. The primary difference is that campus and school administrators need to be involved since they will be operating as instructors as well. In fact, the more training administrators can receive in digital civics and citizenship, the better. Included in this group are librarians, counselors, and other similar staff.

Phase 2

This next phase is a little more hands-off for the facilitator. During this phase, the instructional group decides and plans out how digital civics and citizenship will be taught to their specific participant population. Similarly, extracurricular activities and initiatives are developed and planned. At this point, as much of the staff as possible should be involved in the training and planning.

Phase 2 is where the culture of the learning organization is changed, influenced, and evolved by adding digital civics and citizenship. This is where practice is essential. Faculty and staff practice what they teach. Modeling the traits of advocacy, respect, and education for learners is perhaps the most important lesson that can be conveyed by digital civics and citizenship classes. The same actions and behaviors that are taught and expected for online use are easily translated into physical communication and community within a learning experience.

Phase 3

This final phase of professional development is an extended phase in the sense that it continues for as long as an organization or entity teaches digital civics and citizenship. Phase 3 is a combination of continuing education and training on the content plus individual practice within the learning environment and the larger community. The expectation with this phase is that the learning experience ripples out into the larger community, motivating faculty, staff, and students to become involved in the larger community outside of the school or class.

Given the nature of digital civics and citizenship, phase 3 also includes training on new platforms, apps, and security issues as needed. While teaching, learning, and practicing digital civics and citizenship do not require anyone involved to be an IT expert, it does require individuals to be conversant at a certain level about the digital sphere. An organic and evolving awareness is necessary for instructors to best communicate digital civics and citizenship to learners regardless of the context.

HOLISTIC APPROACH

Perhaps more than any other content area currently taught in K–12 and higher education, digital civics and citizenship requires a holistic approach regardless of the context in which it is taught and learned. *Holistic* is a term bandied about frequently, especially within education and medicine, but it is often misunderstood. For the purposes of this book, *holistic* is defined as "relating to or concerned with wholes or with complete systems rather than with the analysis of, treatment of, or dissection into parts."[1]

An example of this can be found in many of the newer approaches to behavior modification in K–12 schools. Traditionally, if a student misbehaved, the behavior was addressed, and punishment was meted out accordingly. Newer approaches look to establish and cultivate a relationship with students. Instead of simply addressing the misbehavior, teachers look to understand the root causes of the behavior and work with those instead. It may be revealed that the misbehavior was a result of hunger, lack of sleep, anxiety, or a myriad of other influences.

Armed with this knowledge and a broader understanding, the teacher can work with the student to address the situation as best as possible and point out decision-making techniques to the learners that hopefully circumvent future incidences. In essence the teacher is guiding the situation as a life-lesson learning opportunity rather than a simple action-reaction event. Most educators would argue that when this occurs, real teaching and learning are happening. From a digital civics and citizenship perspective, this is true.

In his foundational work *Nicomachean Ethics*, Aristotle famously posited, "Teaching is powerless without a foundation of good habits."[2] This is true for all teaching and learning, especially digital civics and citizenship. Practicing what is taught is essential. The foundation of all authentic learning is understanding. Another classical Greek philosopher is quoted as having said, "The majority of people have no understanding of the things with which they daily meet, nor, when instructed, do they have any right knowledge of them, although to themselves they seem to have."[3]

From early in recorded history, humans have recognized the vital importance of not only practicing what you preach but practicing what you teach. It is crucial that learners in all contexts are provided with instruction and the ability to safely practice the skills they are learning and actively use the knowledge they are being taught under the guidance of an instructor. Our society expects athletes and performers to accept that their passion for play requires regular practice. So why not demand the practice of digital civics and citizenship when it comes to online "play"?

More importantly perhaps is ensuring that the teacher is observed practicing what they teach as well. Educators in traditional settings understand that their lessons extend well beyond the curriculum. Teachers are expected to exhibit and model behavioral and social expectations established by their school. While the administration recognizes that teachers are human, the endeavor of faculty striving to embody the attitudes and behaviors taught is just as important as any lesson from the academic curriculum.

CULTURE AND CLIMATE

Culture in any organization is a key to success. Leaders and managers have known this for decades. In fact, Peter Drucker, the late business management genius, is regularly quoted as saying, "Culture eats strategy for breakfast." While the veracity of this statement continues to be debated in business circles, it is a great cornerstone for the foundation of teaching digital civics and citizenship.

A later chapter in this text explores culture and climate in a learning environment for successfully teaching and practicing digital civics and citizenship. However, a little overview here is helpful. Given the territory already explored in this chapter, the need to address the overall climate and culture in a learning environment is vital. Teaching and learning digital civics and citizenship go hand-in-hand with practicing it, and this is evident in the climate and culture of a school or any other learning organization.

How the culture is created, cultivated, and spread throughout an organization continues to be an area of debate, not only in business circles but also in more traditional academic areas such as anthropology and sociology. Regardless of the details, there are organic ways of cultivating a culture and climate within a learning environment that promote and demonstrate digital civics and citizenship. These are explored in greater depth in a later chapter. However, the two primary organic ways of achieving this are fairly simple. Both are behaviorally based.

The first method is for the instructor to not just model but embody the knowledge and skills of digital civics and citizenship. The second way is for the culture to emerge out of the student population. Both ways are more of a pull than a push, to use "lean" terminology. These terms and their influence on digital civics and citizenship are also explored further in a later chapter.

For our purposes in this chapter, cultivating a *pull* among learners is more desirable than using a *push* method. Exciting curiosity and enabling practice so that students want to learn and develop their digital civics and citizenship aptitude is not only organic, but it fosters lifelong learning as well as practice. To *push* this body of knowledge and skills on learners is to foster short-term learning and memorization for a test. A more in-depth analysis and exploration of push versus pull in teaching digital civics and citizenship can be found in a later chapter exploring climate and culture.

When a learning organization decides to adopt digital civics and citizenship education, it is more than a curricular decision. Unlike some traditional curricula, digital civics and citizenship requires that instructors as well as administrators and other staff members learn and practice the key principles of digital civics and citizenship. This is a vital lesson for learners to experience. In fact, it is key to cultivating authentic learning that extends beyond the classroom.

With an honest analysis of the current climate and culture of the learning organization, the faculty and staff can perform a gap analysis. Having identified the areas that need attention, the entire learning community can strive to bring the climate and culture to a place where digital civics and citizenship can be taught effectively. While this is never an easy task, it is one that will continue to pay benefits. Including as much of the learning community as possible, digital civics and citizenship becomes a transformation tool for the organization.

NOTES

1. https://www.merriam-webster.com/dictionary/holistic.
2. http://classics.mit.edu/Aristotle/nicomachaen.10.x.html.
3. G. T. W. Patrick, trans., *The Fragments of the Work of Heraclitus of Ephesus on Nature* (Baltimore, MD: N. Murray, 1889).

Chapter Ten

Diversity, Inclusion, and Equity in Digital Civics and Citizenship

Current topics of focus in professional and educational operations are diversity, inclusion, and equity. These aspects of learning, development, and practice have raised opponents who harken back to the multicultural education debate that surfaced in the mainstream in the 1980s and 1990s. Regardless of an individual's point of view or opinion on these three areas, they are crucial in fostering learners' success in any content area or skill set.

Given the primacy of these issues within the education industry, many school administrators and community developers are scrambling for learning experiences, curricula, and projects that address diversity, inclusion, and equity within the cultures they are cultivating in their own communities. Digital civics and citizenship is a powerful tool for engaging learners in these areas of knowledge and skills in an authentic and meaningful way. In fact, these three facets of existence in the modern world are deeply and intimately woven into the learning and practice of civics and citizenship, especially in the digital realm.

DIVERSITY

Diversity, especially in education, is a widely debated topic. With the recently renewed focus on it, not only in education but in industry as well, connecting it with digital civics and citizenship is crucial for individuals to create and cultivate a truly civic, complex, and caring society. Diversity and digital civics and citizenship together support and parallel social-emotional learning (SEL). SEL has been explored and analyzed previously in this text.

As with all facets of practicing and teaching digital civics and citizenship, it is important to understand the terms that constitute its working language.

Diversity is part of the bedrock that forms the foundation of a free and democratic society. The current popular understanding of the term *diversity* primarily focuses on an individual's ethnicity, race, socioeconomic status, sexual orientation, identification, and gender. Digital civics and citizenship encapsulates all of these areas and adds several more.

Within the realm of digital civics and citizenship, the focus broadens to include a diversity of perspectives and opinions. In fact, the digital world thrives on a multitude of different opinions, understandings, and points of view. A civil and democratic society not only thrives on this type of diversity but needs it to sustain its overall health and continue to grow. Incorporating digital civics and citizenship into K–12, higher, and community education does two crucial things.

First, civics and citizenship equip individuals with the tools necessary to be citizens not only of their local communities but of the global digital community as well in all its many facets and iterations. Using germ theory [1] as a model of "spreading" the practice of digital civics and citizenship, individuals who attain a working-level mastery of digital civics and citizenship will carry these skills and the supporting knowledge with them into the larger digital and physical world. As a result, these individuals, through their adopted and adapted practices, behaviors, and beliefs, will provide examples of positive digital citizens practicing good digital civics.

Second, building upon the relationship between diversity and digital civics and citizenship, these individuals will move from being examples to taking on the role of informal educators. This understanding also relies on the framework of germ theory, except that in this instance, individuals who are knowledgeable in and practice digital civics and citizenship support and cultivate diversity within their own communities by teaching others. Each practitioner serves as both exemplar and instructor, spreading digital civics and citizenship like a contagion.

INCLUSION

Like diversity, inclusion is a concept held in differing levels of esteem throughout the world. From an education perspective, inclusion has been primarily focused on providing an authentic and open educational experience for students at varying degrees of cognitive development or impairment. The foundation for this was built into then-president Lyndon Johnson's Great Society legislation [2] and was expanded with the Individuals with Disabilities Education Act (IDEA) in 1990. [3]

This discussion reveals not only the definition of the term but also the specific educational practice of including all students in a learning experience regardless of academic ability or intellectual capacity. Building off this understanding, "inclusion" within the teaching, learning, and practice of digital civics and citizenship expands to refer to all learners regardless of demographic identifiers.

As it does with diversity, digital civics and citizenship provides added depth and complexity to inclusion. While it does act upon both the Great Society's and IDEA's understanding of inclusion, digital civics and citizenship instruction and practice focus on inclusion specifically in regard to perspectives and opinions. Like diversity, inclusion in this approach requires allowing a variety of understandings and points of view.

There is a crucial and contentious caveat regarding inclusion and digital civics and citizenship. This caution comes from one of the great Enlightenment thinkers, Voltaire.[4] The quote from Voltaire is discussed in greater depth in the earlier chapters of this text. Regarding our understanding of inclusion, Voltaire's perspective means including not merely dissenting opinions but at times offending opinions. While individuals are allowed and even encouraged to disagree with those offending positions, a policy of inclusion means they can be expressed.

EQUITY

Equity, the last of this contemporary trio, dovetails nicely not only with diversity and inclusion, but also with digital civics and citizenship. For a liberal democracy, defined as a system of government in which individual rights and freedoms are officially recognized and protected and the exercise of political power is limited by the rule of law, in order to work well, equity is necessary. Without it, autocracy and oligarchy emerge to replace democratic rule. All voices are woven together to create the fabric of a democratic nation and a liberal society. For the practice of digital civics and citizenship, equity must be defined workably to understand and appreciate the vital role it plays in this arena.

In the practice of digital civics and citizenship, an integral understanding that must be established is the differentiation between equity and equality. As the first part of the definition of equity states, it is "freedom from bias or favoritism."[5] This is markedly different from equality, which is "the quality or state of being equal."[6] So, while equality will look the same for every individual experiencing it, equity is unique to the individual and the situation itself.

Equity is understood as having the same opportunity within a shared context, whereas equality has everyone starting at the same point with the same attributes and assistance within a shared context. For the practice of digital civics and citizenship, equity is most evident through respectful acts and advocacy among individuals connecting, communicating, and collaborating within the cybersphere.

This means that in the practice of digital civics and citizenship, equity is acknowledged as every individual having the same rights, responsibilities, and opportunities within a shared community. Part of those rights and responsibilities is a shared understanding and upholding of community laws, ordinances, and practices. This is a challenge for some individuals since certain individuals are naturally nonconfrontational.

Equity also includes providing advocacy and support for fellow digital citizens as well as being respectful of them and their opinions. In a metaphorical sense, equity means that everyone has a seat at the proverbial table in practicing digital civics and citizenship. While individuals may have different-sized chairs and sit in different places, those places are theirs.

THE LAW AND THE RULE OF LAW

Regardless of nationality, gender, ethnicity, or any other individual identifier, the landmark United Nations Universal Declaration of Human Rights, adopted in 1948, set forth the foundation for the practice of diversity, inclusion, and equity. The following excerpts from this document speak directly to this topic:

> **Article 6.** Everyone has the right to recognition everywhere as a person before the law.
> **Article 7.** All are equal before the law and are entitled without any discrimination to equal protection of the law. All are entitled to equal protection against any discrimination in violation of this Declaration and against any incitement to such discrimination. [7]

Now, the understanding of "the law" as expressed in the excerpt above must be established. The law and the accompanying phrase "the rule of law" are synonymous in most modern Western societies. These ideas are actually ancient ones that were provided with new and deeper understandings during the Enlightenment. They continue to evolve and adapt as new legal cases are tried in courtrooms around the world.

The Law

In most Western liberal societies where some form of democratic government is practiced, the law plays a crucial part in daily living. The law influences how individuals, citizens and visitors alike, live their lives, work, make decisions, and ultimately engage with the society and government in a civic fashion. The law was first elevated to prominence with the advent of religion. Every faith tradition has a set of rules and rituals that govern the lives of believers.

This tradition changed with the rise of democratic rule and the decline of monarchies and theocracies. With the Protestant Reformation and the various revolutions usurping monarchs, citizens of nations separated religious and secular authority to varying degrees. With the new constitutions that followed, secular law, or common law, was separate from and equal to canon law that governs ecclesiastical matters. The law became something of a separate entity in and of itself.

So, with this understanding, the role of the law in a classically liberal and democratic society can be understood as crucial to digital civics and citizenship. More importantly, it is the law that continues to provide for and protect diversity, inclusion, and equity. This relationship between the law, diversity, inclusion, and equity was established earlier in this chapter.

The Rule of Law

An often-used phrase in government and law is "the rule of law." While most individuals agree to the primary core of this philosophy, most are hard-pressed to provide a working definition or explanation of this phrase. This philosophical understanding and principle of jurisprudence is one of the cornerstones of modern Western democratic societies. One of the best definitions and explanations of practice for the rule of law is provided by the US courts system:

> Rule of law is a principle under which all persons, institutions, and entities are accountable to laws that are:
>
> - publicly promulgated,
> - equally enforced,
> - independently adjudicated, and
> - consistent with international human rights principles. [8]

Certainly, there will be shades of difference between nations and legal systems. However, for the purpose of digital civics and citizenship, this particular understanding of the rule of law is workable. Some key terms in this definition are *public*, *equal*, *independent*, and *human rights*. Each of these terms and how they are brought to life are ingrained within the philosophy and practice of digital civics and citizenship as examined in this text.

The rule of law establishes a set of guiding principles that govern the actions and interactions of individuals within a shared social context. For digital communities, these can be guidelines, expectations, rules, and so on.

Practicing the rule of law within this point of view means that no one person is above these statutes or is absolved from them. All are responsible for following them, protecting them, and enforcing them. The rule of law in this understanding and practice combines the rights of citizenship with the civic responsibilities of every individual. This practice ensures the continuation of a collaborative community while protecting the rights of its members without becoming restrictive and stultifying.

When analyzing conduct and communication in a digital community, the aspects of the rule of law shared here can be used as a rubric to gauge interactions. Doing this creates a dynamic and organic culture within the community of individuals. Discussions and debates regarding the meaning and practice of the terms highlighted foster a collaborative exchange. Similarly, as the community encounters challenges to the understanding of the rule of law, it must collectively address possible changes and amendments based on personal reflection and an understanding of its constituent individuals. These are the actions of a civil society undertaken by its citizenry, regardless of the context.

Adding the ingredients of diversity, inclusion, and equity, along with the law and the rule of law, into the mix for digital civics and citizenship provides a rich and complex product, just like life. Yet these are necessary components for digital civics and citizenship to be not only understood fully but also practiced in a robust and generative manner. These ingredients are vital building blocks to constructing and cultivating a civil society physically and digitally.

INCORPORATING DIVERSITY, INCLUSION, AND EQUITY IN DIGITAL CIVICS AND CITIZENSHIP

The use of currency in the United States has been almost completely replaced by other forms of payment for ease of transaction. However, if we look at any piece of coined or printed money used in the United States, a vital clue to understanding and appreciating the relationship between civics and citizenship and diversity, inclusion, and equity becomes readily apparent.

The Latin phrase "E pluribus unum" can be found on almost every piece of currency used in the United States. This phrase is the motto of the United States and is found on the Great Seal of the United States of America. Translated in English, this phrase means, "Out of many, one." This thirteen-letter Latin phrase continued to be the nation's motto until it was replaced in 1956 with "In God We Trust."

However, it is this original motto that speaks directly both to diversity, inclusion, and equity and to civics and citizenship. History reveals that it was a diversity of voices, ideas, and beliefs that have shaped the nation from its inception. The ebb and flow of diversity, inclusion, and equity is part of the overall narrative of the United States' history. As America's and its citizens' digital footprint increases, it is natural that acknowledging and practicing diversity, inclusion, and equity should follow. However, it must not be assumed.

Building off the basic tenets of Robert's Rules of Order,[9] which offer individuals an orderly framework for sharing and questioning opinions, points of view, and likewise digitally shared information, supports the basic practice of diversity, inclusion, and equity. However, two caveats should be recognized and understood in regard to digital civics and citizenship.

The first of these is the fundamental right to freedom of expression. This aspect has already been explored in depth earlier in this book. For equitable freedom of expression to occur means that there will be messages shared that individuals don't agree with, are offended by, and take issue with. In response to this reality, digital civics and citizenship can guide learners and practitioners to either respond appropriately or move past the offensive message without reply.

If a reply is provided by an individual, they must expect that one of three things will happen. One, no response from the original posting individual will occur. Two, an even more offensive and possibly venomous reply will be given. Or three, the original posting individual will either apologize or make their case for the post. Unfortunately, given the nature of most individuals, the first two responses are the most likely outcomes. Helping individuals realize this through digital civics and citizenship education and practice will help to lessen a lot of the vitriol currently present in the digital realm.

The second caveat can be just as challenging. Given the existence of freedom of expression and what this entails in a democratic society, individuals learning and practicing digital civics and citizenship must acknowledge that there will be some groups in the digital realm that they cannot be a part of. For instance, only veterans can access information and resources from the Veterans Administration. Also, only members of the Freemasons can attend meetings, whether in person or online. This is just the nature of these and similar groups.

Freedom of association coincides with freedom of expression. If groups in the digital realm choose to be exclusive and private, that is their right.

Only if membership is discriminatory with regard to established laws, such as those concerning race, religious affiliation, gender, age, and so forth, does it become incumbent upon individuals to publicly question the validity of the group's existence. As with freedom of expression, individuals who take umbrage toward these exclusive groups must prepare themselves for the possibility that the outcome to any and all challenges may be the exact opposite of what they had hoped for.

Civics and citizenship hinges partially on this truth. In a free and democratic society, at least like those in the West, every individual's opinion holds equal weight. However, should the majority support a point of view counter to a particular individual's opinion, it is up to that individual to recognize that a majority decision, and hopefully a consensus, has been reached. The only restraints are common sense and logic in regard to those decisions. The fundamental rights of life, liberty, and property must be respected to the utmost extent possible.

Much like the American West, the Australian bush, and the South African veldt, the digital sphere is something of a wild and untamed territory. Even though it has been populated for decades, it is still a rough-and-tumble place. Yet history shows that, in the three mentioned physical regions, law and order arose in the nineteenth century from the lives of the pioneers and indigenous peoples who shaped them. Sometimes the law was natural in origin, and at times the order was enforced by a different entity. Regardless, these regions were eventually civilized.

The cybersphere is no different. As recent history has revealed, it is incumbent upon the digital inhabitants to evoke a practice of self-government. Nation-states have legislated and are enforcing external controls over the digital realm in certain parts of the world. In some instances this is good. In others, it is questionable at best. For an authentic liberal democratic society to evolve, laws, ordinances, and practices governing the digital sphere must come from its citizens. It cannot be forced from an external entity.

NOTES

1. V. Nutton, "The Seeds of Disease: An Exploration of Contagion and Infection from the Greeks to the Renaissance," *Medical History* 27, no. 1 (1983): 1–34, https://www.ncbi.nlm.nih.gov/pmc/articles/PMC1139262/?page=23, https://doi.org/10.1017/s0025727300042241.

2. Juan E. Zelizer, *The Fierce Urgency of Now: Lyndon Johnson, Congress, and the Battle for the Great Society* (New York: Penguin, 2015).

3. https://sites.ed.gov/idea/#.

4. E. B. Hall, *The Friends of Voltaire* (London: Putnam, 1907).

5. Ibid.

6. https://www.merriam-webster.com/dictionary/equality.

7. https://www.un.org/en/universal-declaration-human-rights.

8. https://www.uscourts.gov/educational-resources/educational-activities/overview-rule-law.

9. https://www.robertsrules.com.

Chapter Eleven

Teaching Digital Civics and Citizenship

As expressed earlier in the text, instructing individuals in digital civics and citizenship requires superb balance from the teacher. The content of such instruction is a balance between traditional learning and curriculum, on the one hand, and something akin to life skills in practice on the other. From a somewhat humorous point of view, teaching digital civics and citizenship is like a mash-up of social studies and what was once known as home economics, an intriguing combination to say the least.

While this may appear not only strange but impossible at first, upon further consideration it makes sense. Given the robust background that civics and citizenship have, practitioners need to know some of the history involved in these practices. As citizens, regardless of our level of political activity and interest, we are all practitioners of civics and citizenship within the context of where we live and work. There is no escaping it.

Given this mixture of knowledge and skills that digital civics and citizenship encapsulates, the teaching and guiding of students requires agility and adaptability in the instructor. While the content can be standardized and the framework complete, a certain amount of latitude and flexibility must be inherent in the curriculum.

This is due to the nature of the material. The instructor must endeavor to personalize learning as much as possible to the age and education levels of the students. This requires building a collaborative and compassionate culture within the learning space, wherever and whatever that may be. These requirements come as little surprise, considering the experiential and existential nature of digital civics and citizenship.

Part of the challenge of teaching digital civics and citizenship is that the practice itself occurs virtually. In this way, the mere act of participating in digital civics and citizenship expands our understanding of experiential learning and existence. This expanding reality provides educators and learners with challenges. There is little precedent for either group to build upon in the cybersphere.

However, there are some research-based best practices from the traditional learning perspective that can be readily adapted for digital civics and citizenship. They include the following:

- case studies
- problem-based learning
- project-based learning
- a tiered approach

For the purposes of this text, here are the working descriptions for each of these three methods.

CASE STUDIES

The practice of case studies originated in medical education. This activity uses both actual cases and scenarios presented to learners to practice so that instructors can assess their content knowledge and skills as well as their creative and critical-thinking abilities. Anyone who has either worked in health care or has seen television shows and films with doctors and nurses as characters has witnessed case studies in the form of grand rounds, the practice of presenting medical issues and treatments to an audience of doctors, residents, and medical students.

In digital civics and citizenship, teachers can present learners with scenarios in a discussion setting. Keep in mind that this discussion can happen either in person or online. In fact, online is a preferred setting for these discussions since the nature of digital civics and citizenship is virtual.

Like grand rounds, the scenarios that participants encounter should be of varying degrees of complexity. Given the fact that any situation concerning humans already has innate complexities, additional complications often either are not needed or are required only in small doses.

Implementing case studies and scenarios in real time requires preparation on the part of the instructor, as well as a balance between engagement and objectivity during the scenario for all parties involved. The reality of case studies and scenarios can trigger an emotional response for some participants, and even for some instructors. Achieving the desired results takes careful planning and execution, along with some caution.

However, an instructor can easily adopt the two approaches of case studies and scenarios into the learning experience. Case studies are actual events that have taken place, whose actions, consequences, and outcomes are valuable to study as examples. Scenarios, like grand rounds, are live-action and often hypothetical to focus on a specific point. This is an engaging approach to implementing online learning. Learners participate in a scheduled scenario in a controlled online environment where the instructor plays a role similar to a film director or screenwriter on set.

Needless to say, this requires some juggling of roles. As the director or screenwriter, the instructor has either created or adapted a scenario that provides participants with practice. It is up to the instructor, as the creator/adaptor of the scenario, to decide what the outcomes and focuses are for the learners. The focus of the scenario is a good piece of information to share with the whole group prior to commencing the scenario. Doing so keeps the reasons and expectations for the exercise fresh in everyone's mind. Here is an example scenario:

Setting: Present, social media exchange on a popular app/platform.

Topic: Political opinions.

Objective: Engage in a discussion on a particular political topic relevant to current headlines in a civil and constructive manner.

Expectation: Participants communicate with a group, sharing their opinions and perspectives respectfully, without necessarily attempting to persuade or change the opinion of any member of the discussion.

Scenario (to be shared with participants): You are navigating one of your favorite social media apps or platforms when you come across a post that reads as follows: "I can't believe we're still fighting a senseless war in some country that doesn't even like us! We should just pull out and let the locals figure themselves out! I don't care who you are, a *real patriot* would support withdrawing the troops! If you support the war, *then go over there yourself and fight*!!!"

Practice: Students engage the original poster of this quote, and any other replies, in a constructive and civil manner that expresses their opinion and point of view on the topic.

Time: 10–20 minutes.

Guiding Question(s): These are good to start a preview and reflection discussion with the whole group or to assign individually afterward to reflect on the experience.

1. How do we converse civilly about politics with others who may disagree or have differing opinions?
2. What expectations should a participant in this type of dialogue have in mind before becoming actively involved?
3. When should an individual commit to entering, as well as exiting, an exchange such as this?

4. Why would someone want to engage in this type of discussion in the
   first place?

Measurement/Assessment: Since this exercise is subjective in nature,
participants' responses can be assessed by using the definition of civics and citizenship as it applies to communication and exchanges.

Given the relative newness of digital civics and citizenship as a practice and
course of instruction, there are few ready-to-use scenarios for teaching these
skills and their accompanying knowledge. As such, it is incumbent upon
either the instructor or curriculum developer—many times one and the same
person—to develop these scenarios. Thankfully, the media is ripe with examples to build from.

PROBLEM-BASED LEARNING

Problem-based learning is not a new discovery in education. It is neither a
fad nor a trend. In fact, it is very closely related to the case study or scenario
approach. However, the problem-based learning method is one in which
students are either presented with or identify a problem they will address.
Unlike a specific case study or scenario, the majority of problem-based learning experiences look at a situation from a larger perspective.

For example, a case study or scenario may look at an uncivil exchange
between two or more individuals on a social media platform. Participants
examine the causes and effects of the situation and provide possible solutions, interventions, and other actions that could be implemented to successfully resolve the situation.

On the other hand, using problem-based learning challenges students to
take a larger perspective on the situation presented. Perhaps using the same
scenario as explored previously, students could use the problem-based learning approach to identify the larger, underlying problem at the heart of a
particular situation. In this case, it would be the lack of mutual respect that
resulted in an uncivil exchange between the individuals. Participants would
examine the larger problem, investigate possible causes, and propose research-based solutions for alleviating the problem as a whole. Here is an
example of the problem-based learning approach:[1]

Problem: Growing lack of respect and civility in social media exchanges
online.
Task: Provide an evidence-based possible solution that can be effectively
implemented in a noninvasive manner.
Timeline: One calendar year.

Learning Objectives:

- Identify the causes and effects of a social problem.
- Analyze research-based possible solutions.
- Create proposed solutions and ways to implement them.

Learning Outcomes:

- Collaborate with a working group on the assigned problems.
- Present a workable solution.

Measurements:

- Applicability and effectiveness of the proposed solution.
- Adherence to the Wisconsin model for community development.

Scenarios for problem-based learning exist in more abundance than specific digital-sphere case studies and scenarios, so there is more material for instructors to use in educational experiences. The challenge with this learning method is clearly in defining the outcomes and measurements. Given the nature of this learning experience, it is crucial that these be real-world in nature.

PROJECT-BASED LEARNING

Project-based learning parallels the problem-based learning method in many ways. Both challenge students to address a particular issue and create a workable solution to be presented. However, as their names suggest, the focus of the two differs. This results in a different point of view and approach to the experience for all involved.

For the purposes of this text, project-based learning can be understood as a learning experience in which learners focus on a particular project that addresses a need for a group or community. Participants must provide a viable solution, with possible alternatives, addressing this identified need. The solution, or solutions, must not only be practical but also supported by research.

Like problem-based learning, this approach can borrow from actual issues that the participants' community is facing. In fact, utilizing these issues and needs can provide a depth of relevancy and realism to the learning experience that no concocted scenario could ever hope to have. As such, it is highly recommended that digital civics and citizenship instructors who are planning on implementing project-based learning be familiar with the issues and needs facing the learners' community. Here is an example of a project-based learning experience:

Topic: Instructing online community members in the effective practices of digital civics and citizenship.

Learning Objectives:

- Identify and explain the need for this form of community education.
- Analyze the potential impact of teaching digital civics and citizenship.
- Create a proposed plan(s) for offering the necessary education to the community.

Learning Outcomes:

- Provide evidence supporting the need for digital civics and citizenship community education.
- Produce a plausible plan(s) for implementing digital civics and citizenship education, with an understanding of lifelong learning.

Measurements/Assessments:

- Applicability of proposed plan(s) within the community.
- Impact of proposed plan(s) on the community.

Project-based learning can be understood as similar to the real-world final stages of approaching a need or issue facing a community. This method of experiential learning closely resembles the actions taken by professionals in public service as well as in private industry. In fact, this action is a major part of the founding philosophy that supports project-based learning.

TIERED APPROACH

Reading through this chapter may have made clear that the three methods presented here dovetail with one another. This is intentional. All three methods can be employed within the digital civics and citizenship curriculum in a tiered approach to learning. In fact, this tiered approach has been implemented in other content areas in more formal learning contexts with positive results.

Using this tiered approach, instructors guide students through the levels of mastery in digital civics and citizenship. Starting with case studies or scenarios, learners have an opportunity to examine the topic through real-world examples. Dipping into traditional background knowledge regularly while navigating these scenarios provides relevancy. The scenarios themselves add a facet of immediacy to the learning.

Based on the scenario experience, learners identify the larger problems at the root of issues. Learners build from their acquired knowledge and skills from the scenarios to identify the problems and propose solutions. From a solution endpoint in the problem-based learning phase, learners then move on to a larger-scope approach with the project-based learning experience.

Ending the learning experience with the project-based phase works along the guidelines for community education and development established by the Wisconsin model. As a result, individual community members collectively contribute possible solutions to the problem that was first identified at the end of the first phase and grappled with in the second phase of the learning experience.

In fact, this tiered approach can also serve as a useful tool in articulating the learning experiences for participants, both prospective and actual. Regardless of the context in which digital civics and citizenship instruction is provided, this tiered approach can help differentiate the levels of instruction. For example, the case study approach could be used in the beginning-level class, or basic course. Then learners can matriculate to a second level, or intermediate course, that utilizes problem-based learning, and then on to an advanced course with the project-based approach. Utilizing this tiered method provides a way for learners and instructors to effectively build upon their experiences in the previous level.

ASSESSING LEARNER COMPETENCY

With any learning, measuring the learner's acquisition of new knowledge and skills is traditionally the end of the learning experience. Instructors and institutions measure their own success by the competency of their learners as displayed on tests and exams, at least in a traditional learning environment. However, while much of digital civics and citizenship is founded upon traditional knowledge and practices, it is itself a nontraditional practice.

Digital civics and citizenship by its very nature is a practice, a daily understanding of community and interpersonal interactions. Its nature has been explored and examined throughout this text. As such, using traditional measurements and assessments will not provide a complete picture of an individual's competency in digital civics and citizenship. It will, however, provide a baseline measurement. As shown earlier in this chapter, a mixture of traditional and alternative assessments provides learners and educators with a more honest measurement of competency and mastery. It's the nontraditional portion of measurement that is the most challenging for educators.

The simplest means of conducting this part of the assessment is observation. In K–12 and even in the higher educational spheres, this is somewhat easy. In a K–12 setting, educators observe and interact with learners more easily given the nature and structure of the overall learning endeavor. In higher education, this becomes a little more challenging. Shifting to the realm of community education, this form of measurement is almost impossible.

Surveys are powerful tools for assessing the mastery and practice of digital civics and citizenship in all three of these realms of teaching and learning. Given the fact that surveys can now be delivered almost effortlessly online, engaging learners in self-reflection through a mixed, online survey can provide instructors with vital and current information. Follow-ups of initial learning surveys can also provide both in-depth as well as longitudinal data. This information yields insights into a program's efficacy. It also opens up discussions regarding revision and updating needs.

It is crucial for educators and administrators as well as learners to understand and appreciate that the learning and practice of digital civics and citizenship will always be an ongoing effort. As such, it is incumbent upon each individual to use self-reflection in order to measure their progress once the planned learning experience is completed. Keeping this in mind, learners at all stages can endeavor to continue increasing their mastery, while challenging others to learn, practice, and promote digital civics and citizenship.

When dealing with community education, one of the essential factors in a program's or initiative's success is participant buy-in and engagement. Unlike K–12 or higher education, individuals are neither required nor traditionally rewarded for participating in community education programs. Personal edification and posterity are no longer the draws they once were in getting citizens interested and involved in local government. However, the following approach to introducing and integrating digital civics and citizenship through community education programs and initiatives may be a tool for increasing citizen participation and engagement within the local community.

Positive rewards are a powerful way to engage learners and cultivate continued progress. This time-tested approach of positive reinforcement can be used within the realm of community education in order to promote the learning and practice of digital civics and citizenship. Also, this approach can increase citizens' awareness and engagement with local government and agencies in a more positive fashion.

The following method is provided as an example of implementing digital civics and citizenship in a community education setting.

PHASE 1

Using the local library and community centers, initiate a multitiered approach to digital civics and citizenship instruction and practice. This multitiered approach would have instructional and practice sessions offered in the three primary modes. These are traditional, hybrid, and fully digital. The traditional mode is just what it sounds like. This educational setting is a classroom of some sort populated by learners led by an instructor. The hybrid balances the learning experience seamlessly between in-person and online learning experiences. The fully digital learning experience is completely on-line.

Individuals will be motivated to attend and complete these introductory learning experiences and practice sessions through the rewards system. Along with being asked to function as community leaders and trainers in the digital civics and citizenship initiative, points will be awarded as well. These points can be used in a variety of ways, including the following:

- reduction of library fines
- special digital sessions with community government leaders
- public recognition

This approach encourages participation by individual citizens. These methods do not punish citizens who opt out of participating but rather positively encourage those who do engage.

PHASE 2

In this follow-up phase, the focus is on leveraging the individuals who became engaged in phase 1 to become community civics and citizenship leaders. These individuals will be guided in becoming digital civics and citizenship instructors and embedded small-group leaders within their own local communities. Again, the primary goal of digital civics and citizenship instruction is to equip individuals with the tools they need to interact civilly in the digital realm. The initiative is nonpartisan.

This phase should also see individuals from the first phase possibly entering into local politics, either through election or appointment. Also, using a tool such as customer satisfaction surveys for citizens, coupled with similar measurements for civil servants, could show an increase in positive responses. The efforts of digital civics and citizenship in this area may result in a change of digital climate and culture to a more civil atmosphere initiated by the end users.

PHASE 3

This final and continuing phase is primarily focused on continued cultivation, interest, and activity among individual citizens. For a municipal or county governmental entity, this requires regular contact, updates, and revision of digital communications, interactions, and opportunities for community growth. At some point, either in this phase or in the one before it, a team or perhaps an entire department should be established with the responsibility of cultivating this civil digital community.

Creating a permanent department, office, or team within the local government with the responsibility of fostering digital civics and citizenship should not necessarily have a large cost to it. In fact, this collection of professionals can be a key piece in creating and sustaining interorganizational cooperation within local government. In doing so, municipal agencies can provide a more holistic and integrated experience for citizens.

For example, most cities and counties have a chamber of commerce, a tourism bureau, a public library, a public health office, and other such entities that focus on outreach to the community. By combining efforts from these different departments and organizations and bringing together their talents and experience to focus on digital civics and citizenship, the majority of the expense incurred is for citizen engagement and empowerment.

Once a community has undertaken this initiative and has seen some success, it can leverage its connections with its "sister cities" if the community participates in such a program. If it does, then the instruction and practice of digital civics and citizenship organically becomes a geopolitical initiative shared between governmental entities and their constituent citizens. Doing so adds depth to the environmental slogan "Think Global, Act Local."

An activity that can assist in building a robust digital, civil community that is both engaging and welcoming is an adapted form of scavenger hunt. This activity can provide myriad results for the global digital audience. From a more local standpoint, this activity can offer residents, new and old, the chance to get to know not only the departments, agencies, and organizations within their local government but also the individuals who staff them.

On a more global scale, the scavenger hunt activity allows the larger audience to digitally explore the municipality. Doing so can lead to closer ties between the citizens of sister cities as they encounter one another in this activity and digitally explore their native cities together.

This digital scavenger hunt can provide other rewards as well. As examined earlier, a point system can be established. Based on interactions with other digital citizens, the civic actions and attitudes displayed online, as well as online engagement with the different organizations, departments, and agencies within the municipality, can result in points being awarded. Likewise, these points can be used not only to identify active citizens but also to reward individual citizens with unique civic privileges.

This digital scavenger hunt will look different in each context it's utilized in. However, regardless of the implementation, the results should be very similar across communities. This activity is also a great way to involve local businesses in recruiting new employees as well as to attract new businesses.

Through the digital scavenger hunt, a municipality would increase the sense of "community" among its citizens while also prospecting for potential new citizens.

The three instructional approaches and methodologies provided in this chapter are not only research based, with decades of evidence supporting their implementation, but are also counted among best practices by the majority of educators across the industry. These tiered methods provide participants the opportunity to not only work on relevant issues associated with the topic but to also make deeper connections between each phase of the learning experience, the importance of the acquired knowledge and skills, and their own individual roles in the larger process. Teaching and learning digital civics and citizenship in this way promotes participatory democracy and civic engagement, both of which are crucial facets of digital civics and citizenship.

NOTE

1. Wisconsin Module for Community Development, https://dpi.wi.gov/community-education/components.

Chapter Twelve

Integrating with the STEM/STEAM Curriculum

Within the current spectrum of PK–20 education in the United States is STEM (science, technology, engineering, and mathematics). A growing need for skilled professionals in these disciplines has motivated a variety of national educational initiatives, ranging from curriculum development to scholarships and research grants aimed at increasing studies in these areas.

One of the first adaptations of this STEM surge was to ensure that the arts were not forgotten, and STEM evolved into STEAM (science, technology, engineering, the arts, and mathematics). There is a wealth of data to show the connection between the arts and the sciences to support this concerted inclusion of the arts in STEAM.

Yet the enigma of organically positioning digital civics and citizenship within STEM and STEAM curricula still needs to be riddled out to a workable solution for instructors and learners. A working understanding of how these approaches address learning needs helps educators understand how to incorporate digital civics and citizenship into these curricula.

STEM CURRICULUM

The STEM curriculum, which regularly finds its way into campaign speeches and media headlines, is a mainstay of education in the United States. Something similar to STEM was experienced in the United States at the end of World War II and the advent of the Cold War. American public schools and universities put a renewed and increased emphasis on the sciences, especially engineering. This focus was fully supported by the federal government, as evidenced in a white paper written by Vannevar Bush.[1] This push was motivated not only by the desire to help the United States win the space race, but also to protect it technologically from communism.

The fervor that resulted helped to create the legion of scientists and engineers who were responsible not only for getting American astronauts to the moon but also for the space shuttle program. It even laid the groundwork for the International Space Station. And it spawned developments that many individuals enjoy, such as wireless headsets, water filtration, hybrid automobiles, solar-generated electricity, and many others that are results of this push in the 1950s and 1960s.

The personal computer revolution in the 1970s and 1980s carried this initiative further, but the fervor quickly calmed to cool embers. The dot-com and subsequent digital revolution added some fuel to the faintly glowing embers. However, this was not enough. Recent political campaigns and research by nongovernmental organizations have revealed that US infrastructure is in need of repair and upgrade. This, along with facets of the nation's health care, manufacturing, and other industries, cries out in need for a new generation of scientists, engineers, and researchers.

STEAM CURRICULUM

Theoretically, STEAM provides an equal footing for the arts among the sciences. As computing expanded and grew in complexity with the advent of digital technology, and as it continues with quantum computing, the sciences began to embrace the tools and perspectives traditionally ensconced within the arts. Terms like *mood* were now needed in order to describe newly identified subatomic particles and their movements for physicists to begin to communicate their discoveries and their theories.

Higher-order mathematics such as fractals and other discrete mathematical occurrences are now commonplace in the working parlance of scientists and mathematics. Since these do not necessarily "fit" within the traditional mechanical understanding of the universe and its workings, they are often conveyed by new terms, different perspectives, and what would be understood as nontraditional techniques. This is where the arts come into play.

Physicist Fritjof Capra was one of the early promoters of this combination with many of his popular science books. These include *The Tao of Physics*, *The Web of Life*, and many others. Capra combined his scientific profession with his passion for Eastern culture, history, and religions to engage nonscientists with his writings and share his ideas and theories about the nature of the universe.

Many other scientists have adopted this approach. However, for digital civics and citizenship and the STEAM curriculum, trying to impose this approach in a cookie-cutter fashion will not work. This method, though, can inform and influence the inclusion of digital civics and citizenship into an established STEAM curriculum.

INTEGRATING DIGITAL CIVICS
AND CITIZENSHIP WITH STEAM

At first glance, integrating digital civics and citizenship into either STEM or STEAM curricula may appear counterintuitive. However, taking into account the history of both science and civics and citizenship, a connection between these becomes more apparent.

Engineering, mathematics, and the sciences all work within a shared framework. This framework is known most commonly as the scientific method. This process requires individuals to investigate problems, ask questions, and perform experiments rationally and objectively. The scientific method also calls for a free exchange of information and collaborative communication from practitioners. These same facets also are fundamental practices of government in a democratic society. Rationality and reason are keys in this understanding.

When looking at the evolution and practice of civics and citizenship in Western history, rationality and reason were the progenitors of equality among individuals. Objective reasoning provided the foundation for understanding the significance of each individual citizen, while balancing this with the responsibility of individual citizens to execute their civic duties within a democratic society.

Similarly, it was modern liberal societies, democratic for their time, that were the fertile soil in which the Scientific Revolution and the Industrial Revolution blossomed and came to full fruition, advancing Western society. And like a closed feedback loop, the advances in science influenced the political thinking of many great individuals. The founders of America, such as Thomas Jefferson and Benjamin Franklin, were profoundly influenced and inspired by these new ways of looking at and understanding the universe and its workings. This is evident in the writings produced by this group. These include the Declaration of Independence and the Constitution of the United States.

Implementing digital civics and citizenship practices within the STEM and STEAM curricula is more practical and experiential than teaching it in a stand-alone setting, complementing the previous methods explored in earlier chapters. Again, the scientific method provides not only an entry point for the inclusion of digital civics and citizenship but also a rationale in defense of it as well.

The following list provides some suggested activities that teachers can use to have students recognize the relationship between digital civics and citizenship and STEM/STEAM.

DISCUSSION

Set parameters, objectives, and expected outcomes for this activity; communicate these at the outset; and have a moderator enforce them. Otherwise, what seems like a simple activity can grow into an uncontrolled experience.

Scenario #1

Students will discuss a particular STEM topic, such as solar power or wind power, over a video conferencing platform or a discussion board such as Reddit that is closely monitored for safety, security, and privacy. Students will use research and their own experimentation as evidence.

Assessment #1

Instructors are encouraged to use a modified or adapted Wisconsin model for an assessment framework. While these learning experiences cannot sufficiently address all aspects of the model, it is recommended that the instructor select two or three of these aspects to focus on. This modification can be taken further with the instructor regularly rotating in new aspects from the model to replace ones already used.

Debate #1

This is a natural progression and partner of discussion. Where discussion provides learners the opportunity to explore the issue or topic in an open and relatively safe environment, debate challenges them to examine a certain aspect or facet and to defend their particular understanding and point of view.

Scenario #2

Students will debate the pros and cons of a particular STEM topic, such as solar power or wind power, over a video conferencing platform or a discussion board such as Reddit. Students will use research and their own experimentation as support for their stance. The civic facet of the debate will be the tax incentives for alternative power sources and increased taxes on producers and consumers of traditional power.

Assessment #2

Instructors are encouraged to use a modified or adapted Wisconsin model for an assessment framework. While these learning experiences cannot sufficiently address all aspects of the model, it is recommended that the instructor select two or three of these aspects to focus on. This modification can be taken further with the instructor regularly rotating in new aspects from the model to replace ones already used. Along with this, the instructor should include equal weight for the preparation and delivery of the debate.

DEVELOPMENT

The third D in the integration of STEM/STEAM within digital civics and citizenship is development. It is a natural progression from the previous two steps. Learners are taking the knowledge they have obtained through research and the skills they have honed through debate to develop a proposal that promotes community development. The topic is STEM/STEAM based and has immediate applicability in the local community.

Scenario

Students will debate the pros and cons of a particular STEM topic, such as solar power or wind power, over a video conferencing platform, or even using a discussion board such as Reddit. Students will use research and their own experimentation as support for their stance. The civic facet of the debate is a civic development plan, such as changing over the local power source to being either entirely or predominantly solar or wind.

Assessment

Instructors are encouraged to use a modified or adapted Wisconsin model for an assessment framework. While these learning experiences cannot sufficiently address all aspects of the model, it is recommended that the instructor select two to three of these aspects to focus on. This modification can be taken further with the instructor regularly rotating in new aspects from the model to replace ones already used. Along with this, the instructor should include equal weight for the development, presentation, and delivery of the proposal.

These three options are just that—options or suggestions. In learning and development, a certain amount of flexibility is required. In fact, one of the best practices to prepare instructors as well as learners for this latitude is the art of improv. This is a topic for another, more in-depth discussion. However, many effective educators find that improv is worth some research and experimentation.

One of the hidden gems of education that these suggestions reveal is creativity. Creative thinking is a key component of learning and development that is gaining credence in the current culture as the world becomes more agile and as disruption is more the rule than the exception. Being able to quickly adapt and improvise are key traits that an individual needs to be successful in their professional and private lives.

ASSESSMENTS AND MEASUREMENTS

In the examples provided above, suggestions were made for measurements and assessments to identify learners' mastery and competence. However, what has not been fully addressed is the understanding and appreciation in regard to measurements and assessments in teaching digital civics and citizenship. Having the right or proper mind-set and perspective regarding assessing learners, the measurement tools employed, and the data collected is all part of the teaching mind-set.

The existential nature of teaching and learning digital civics and citizenship challenges educators to move beyond traditional forms of assessment and measurement. Traditional tests and quizzes can be used in this learning environment. However, they will only provide data about learners' foundational knowledge concerning the history and influences of digital civics and citizenship. In other words, traditional assessments and measurements can only supply data regarding learners' comprehension of the *why* and *what* of the content.

STEM and STEAM curricula are focused primarily on problem solving, critical and creative thinking, and analysis. They are also experientially focused on the traditional content areas of math and science. As such, the assessments and measurements are applied in natural settings.

Educators should follow this approach when incorporating digital civics and citizenship into STEM and STEAM learning environments and experiences. In doing so, the instructor plays a double role of not only a teacher assessing and measuring students, but also a field researcher observing the exchanges between learners and the efficacy of their collaboration.

This means that the instructor must take an active role in measuring and assessing their students. In order to do this effectively, the instructor needs to actively observe and engage the students as they are practicing and while they are being assessed. These measurements along with passive observations provide a deeper and more nuanced understanding of learners' comprehension and competency regarding digital civics and citizenship. Instructors can actually witness and participate in learning experiences with the students in order to obtain measurement data to assess their learning.

Learning and teaching are no different. Instructors are challenged to know their learners as well as possible. Understanding what learners bring with them into the classroom, such as experiences, points of view, and other similar attributes, helps instructors better tailor or adapt the learning experiences provided. This aspect of teaching is perhaps one of the most important as well as challenging parts of education.

Integrating digital civics and citizenship into an established STEM/STEAM curriculum is not necessarily difficult, but it may not be easy either. What's required is broadening the scope of understanding regarding what STEM and STEAM curricula encompass. In spite of the focus indicated by their names, the other content areas are neither ignored nor left out. In fact, it could be argued that the humanities and other knowledge areas play roles just as important as the sciences in STEM and STEAM education. The only shift is that the sciences play the leading role in STEM and STEAM.

Given the fact that digital civics and citizenship is steeped in experiential learning, it actually provides additional depth to STEM and STEAM curricula. The arena of digital civics and citizenship challenges learners to operate in real-world roles using the methods and activities provided in this chapter. As such, incorporating digital civics and citizenship into an existing STEM/STEAM curriculum is a research-based best practice for engaging learners by making the content real and applicable to their daily lives and individual interests.

More than anything, digital civics and citizenship education challenges instructors and learners to experiment. Even if a participant attains all of the historical, philosophical, and conceptual knowledge that supports and shapes digital civics and citizenship, without application through practice it becomes stagnant knowledge. Regardless of the context, digital civics and citizenship is experiential. Its regular utilization leads to the fullness of the practice and the accompanying philosophy.

NOTE

1. Vannevar Bush, *Science, the Endless Frontier* (Washington, DC: US Government Printing Office, 1945), https://www.nsf.gov/od/lpa/nsf50/vbush1945.htm.

Chapter Thirteen

Integrating Digital Civics and Citizenship with a Traditional Curriculum

Even with the increased focus on science, technology, engineering, and mathematics (STEM), as well as science, technology, engineering, arts, and mathematics (STEAM), there are numerous educational entities and organizations that have chosen either not to make this approach the main focus or to return to a more traditional content curriculum and approach to teaching and learning. Here, too, digital civics and citizenship needs to be integrated into daily learning activities. This chapter focuses on how to authentically embed digital civics and citizenship into a traditional teaching and learning curriculum, approach, and environment.

While integrating digital civics and citizenship into a traditional curriculum and learning environment may seem intuitive, it actually presents just as problematic a challenge as it does within a STEM/STEAM-focused setting. However, it can be accomplished successfully. In some of the ways that are explored in this chapter, integrating digital civics and citizenship into a traditional curriculum and learning environment complements traditional learning experiences by adding depth and complexity.

The traditional curriculum includes four primary or core content areas: math, science, language arts and literature, and social studies. Given that the STEM/STEAM chapter has already provided examples and recommendations for the sciences, this chapter examines the subject areas of social studies and language arts/literature. Along with these two content areas, this chapter further explores the arts and offers recommendations for learning experiences. For ease of implementation by the instructor, the recommendations in all areas have similarities.

SOCIAL STUDIES

Of all the traditional content areas, social studies seems to be the perfect subject to have digital civics and citizenship accompany it through the entire learning experience cycle.

However, even though some states have embedded the federal citizenship test within the social studies curriculum, they require little if any civics or citizenship education to actually be taught. This is true even in the states in which students must pass the federal exam as part of their high school graduation requirements.

Earlier chapters explored some of the reasons behind the retreat from civics and citizenship education. Even a renewed focus on these subject areas primarily exposes learners to very basic concepts, such as voting, representation, the Declaration of Independence, the US Constitution, and other similar facets. There is seldom exposure to the behavioral aspects of civics and citizenship, especially regarding the digital environment.

People and events throughout history provide ample opportunities to discuss civics and citizenship in practice. Educators can mine some, if not most, historical figures and episodes and easily adapt them to digital scenarios to discuss with students. Similar to the case studies method examined in a previous chapter, analyzing episodes from history within the framework of civics and citizenship allows learners and the instructor to examine cyberspace practices and behaviors from an objective point of view. In doing this, attitudes, behaviors, points of view, and opinions can be analyzed in a way that allows for rational analysis with little if any emotional reaction from those involved.

Example: "Tweeting Rosa Parks" Scenario

Rosa Parks is carrying out her bus sit-in. She is live-tweeting her experience, with photos and videos, from her cell phone while she refuses to move to the back of the segregated bus, as the law at that time required. Parks sees a surge of popular support for her social media posts, as well as an equal amount of backlash, from people around the world.

Activity

Learners create their own social media posts in response not only to posts by Rosa Parks but also to reactions from other individuals. Student responses can take the form of any of the available social media platforms. Learners will create three unique posts comprising one wholly original post, one response to a post by Parks, and one response to a negative reply to Parks.

Instructor Preparation

For this activity to achieve its objectives, the instructor must prepare some social media posts beforehand. These include posts by Rosa Parks as well as some responses and replies from outside of the learning group. The negative replies should be edgy and border on offensive but not cross the line. The goal is to prompt practice from learners, not to provoke emotional responses.

Application

When guiding learners through this experience, it is recommended that the flow should be guided as follows, as naturally as possible:

Introduction

The instructor should conduct an informal, oral assessment to gauge learners' knowledge of Rosa Parks, the civil rights movement, and the Montgomery bus boycott. Use verified sites to have students fill in any knowledge gaps the group may have.

The instructor provides an overview of the exercise and reminds participants of their responsibilities and the expectations for the exercise. Also, the instructor reviews the assessment framework (modified Wisconsin model) by which their interactions will be measured.

Activity

Students encounter and engage with the social media posts generated by the instructor. They then create the minimum requisite posts, responses, and replies. While students are composing these, it is recommended that the instructor engage learners individually about their feelings, thoughts, and how they would like to respond, as well as how to honestly voice their opinion(s) in a civil manner, with the Wisconsin model used as a guideline.

Reflection

To provide closure to this learning experience, the instructor can bring the participants together as a whole group. Learners can share some of their posts with the group for constructive feedback. Facilitating the discussion, the instructor needs to regularly assess the participants' posts with the group using the Wisconsin model. As part of this debriefing, the instructor should also allow participants to share their experience and challenge them to analyze their own individual reactions and responses.

Summary

While this learning activity is focused on a very public act and the ensuing responses, it is equally based upon individual interactions. This challenges participants, including the instructor, to deftly balance between an individual's right to freedom of expression and the civic good and responsibilities of a citizen within the larger community. Such a situation is something that citizens grapple with regularly.

This and similar scenarios provide students with the ability to experience one of these situations within the safe parameters of a learning environment. It also provides learners with the opportunity to gauge their interactions in a framework of expectations. Learners are also provided with an opportunity to receive peer feedback in a constructive environment.

LANGUAGE ARTS AND LITERATURE

The skills included in the language arts and literature content area include reading, writing, spelling, grammar, and speech. Some would argue, possibly correctly, that this content area is the most important of all the traditional core competencies taught in the majority of schools. That debate is for another time and place.

The content area of language arts and literature provides a wide vista for integrating digital civics and citizenship. Earlier in this text, the necessity of communication and free speech in all its forms was established. Just by reviewing the essential components of language arts and literature with this in mind reveals the strong connection between these two content areas. Yet this ease of connection belies the fact that embedding digital civics and citizenship within language arts and literature is challenging.

Following is a recommended learning experience that provides the opportunity for learners to practice their civics and citizenship skills digitally, as well as to better understand the deeply held connection between language arts and digital civics and citizenship.

Example: Living Languages

For citizens around the world, language is the common currency, even though it is used in different forms and denominations. Knowing how to use this social currency and leverage its credit is essential for daily life. This is especially true within the area of government and politics. A citizen of any country must understand and appreciate the nuances of the local language, the lingua franca, to communicate and comprehend effectively.

In this learning experience, participants parse, deconstruct, and respond civilly to social media posts from government agencies, elected and appointed representatives, and other entities involved in government. The primary goal of this experience is to examine and appreciate how language is used and misused by the government. The result is a heightened awareness and deeper understanding of the power of language and its centrality to practicing civics and citizenship.

Scenario

The instructor selects three to five social media posts from a variety of platforms. These posts should be from individual government agencies, elected representatives, political pundits, and so on. They should come from government at as wide a variety of levels as possible: local, state, federal, and international. Share these posts with the whole group of participants.

Activity

Whole group: Read and review the posts. Identify their source. Then parse the message. Take apart not only the message but its constituent words.

Small groups: Assign each group one of the posts. Have the members of each group research some of the background of the posts' sources (e.g., platform, function, responsibilities). Members will research the constituent parts of the post they were assigned, paying close attention to the words used.

Whole group: A spokesperson for each group will report back their group's analysis and findings. The focus will be on what the central message of the post was intended to be.

Small groups: Group members will revise and rewrite the posts to better communicate the identified central message.

Whole group: A spokesperson from each group will share their group's revision. The instructor will then lead a whole group discussion looking critically at the original and revised messages for which best communicates the intended message, then follow up with an analysis of why the post's originator possibly chose the language and words they did.

Assessment/Measurement

The entire group, assisted by the instructor, will assess the social media posts as well as their revision using the Wisconsin model. This assessment can be extended by critiquing the original and revised posts against the civic virtues enumerated and defined by Aristotle. These can be found earlier in the text. The final part of the assessment is to have participants reflect on the experience and report how it has changed their understanding of political and civic communication.

Summary

This is a challenging and possibly even difficult learning experience, but it is an opportunity to learn and practice crucial skills for civics and citizenship. This is especially true in the digital realm, where communication with government and elected officials is easier. Effective communication, the sending and receiving of messages, is a foundational part of civics and citizenship. Thomas Jefferson elucidated this truth when he wrote to Richard Price in 1789, saying that "wherever the people are well informed they can be trusted with their own government."[1]

It is incumbent upon the instructor to improvise and adapt this learning experience, mostly on the spot, to engage the participants as much as possible. To assist in this, educators can use both Piaget's theory of cognitive development[2] and Kohlberg's theory of moral development.[3] These two frameworks of human development provide guideposts for adapting learning experiences that the instructor can use to balance engagement and challenge for learners.

Embedding digital civics and citizenship learning experiences into a traditional curriculum through social studies and language arts and literature is somewhat more straightforward compared to STEM/STEAM learning approaches. These two traditional content areas are more open to weaving digital civics and citizenship into learning experiences. Both social studies and the language arts and literature provide arenas for learners to understand the background of civic responsibilities and the rights of citizenship, as well as the importance of clear and informed communication within the realm of government and politics.

While some individuals and groups may object to the close association of digital civics and citizenship with government and politics, separation is nearly impossible. Civics and citizenship, whether digital or traditional, inform and shape government and politics. The larger question of which came first is something of a non sequitur for the purposes of this text.

The key to successful implementation and embedding digital civics and citizenship into more traditional curricula is application of the knowledge and skills in scenarios that are digital in nature. This means that a digital dimension must be added to the learning experience. Doing so is antithetical to a traditional curriculum. However, it does add an opportunity for learners to experiment with digital civics and citizenship in a controlled and safe environment.

Perhaps the greatest challenge in embedding digital civics and citizenship within social studies and language arts and literature is for the instructor. To make the learning experience as authentic and fulfilling as possible for the participants, the instructor must fiercely maintain as objective a stance as possible. Similar to a scientific experiment, the environment must be as "clean" as possible in order to guard against "contaminants." Regarding the learning and practice of digital civics and citizenship, instructors must teach and model identifying their own biases and setting them aside.

Similarly, learning organizations that have adopted digital civics and citizenship in place of the traditional curriculum must appreciate the distinction between curriculum and instruction. In many cases, learning organizations that label themselves as "traditional" adopt a lecture-style instruction method. However, this is not necessarily traditional curriculum. As such, the push-back coming from these organizations stems in part from this misunderstanding. Just as imbedding digital civics and citizenship into the traditional social studies curriculum challenges instructors to maintain a base level of objectivity and equity in regard to points of view and opinions, it also challenges institutions and organizations to differentiate their understanding of curriculum versus instruction.

Imbedding digital civics and citizenship into the traditional curriculum can be challenging but can also add greater depth and complexity to the overall learning experience. This is evident in the examples provided earlier in this chapter. Moving debates, discussions, and collaborations into the digital realm removes many of the traditional barriers instructors grapple with. These include time and location, as well as others. Moving learning experiences into the digital sphere is a natural way of extending learning. Practice in digital civics and citizenship provides students with a framework for learning within this context.

NOTES

1. https://www.loc.gov/exhibits/jefferson/60.html.

2. Bärbel Inhelder and Jean Piaget, *The Growth of Logical Thinking from Childhood to Adolescence* (New York: Basic Books, 1958).

3. Lawrence Kohlberg, *The Psychology of Moral Development: The Nature and Validity of Moral Stages*, vol. 2 of *Essays on Moral Development* (San Francisco: Harper & Row, 1984).

Chapter Fourteen

Stand-Alone Learning Experiences

Using stand-alone courses to teach digital civics and citizenship is seldom examined or practiced. Traditionally in K–12 education in the United States, civics and citizenship courses were at one time offered as stand-alone classes within the larger curriculum. When it comes to digital civics and citizenship, this approach is not only viable but even recommended in certain contexts. This chapter explores the stand-alone approach and includes recommendations for conducting digital civics and citizenship instruction in this manner, as well as recommended contexts for having stand-alone courses for this topic.

Looking at how traditional civics and citizenship classes are taught and what was covered in them can help to inform and guide digital civics and citizenship instruction. As stated previously, the insight, knowledge, and wisdom gleaned from examining traditional civics and citizenship education doubly informed the purpose of this text. First, it serves to identify what knowledge and skills are essential and which methods of instruction have been used to best communicate the content. Second, it helps to reflect on which methods are no longer applicable due to technology, information, perspective, and understanding.

Both points of view are important. However, it is best to approach the second one first. It is crucial for digital civics and citizenship educators to identify outdated perspectives and opinions, such as those that are nationalistic, within traditional civics and citizenship education. These must be removed from the curriculum. If they cannot be easily removed or are brought up by learners, they must be addressed openly and candidly. Doing this is fundamental to create a successful learning environment for participants.

CURRICULUM

In any planned learning experience, identifying the best curriculum is always a challenge. Typically, instructors have two options. The first is to shop around for the best available curriculum created by a third-party vendor. This is what most formal educational institutions do. There is nothing wrong with an organization going this route for digital civics and citizenship education. In fact, this option may be the best one to get a program started and help it build momentum within whatever community or context where it is being utilized.

With the surge in civics and citizenship education continuing throughout the United States, there are vendors who provide a ready-made curriculum. However, there are few if any established curricula offered by vendors that focus on digital civics and citizenship education with a global perspective. This gap may be addressed by educational publishers in the future.

When educators do find a ready-made curriculum, history provides evidence that curricula generated by third parties have their own pros and cons. These include the materials provided, learning activities, assessments, and the adaptability of the curriculum. These aspects are part of the review and recommendation process that educators and administrators go through when the time comes for purchasing a new curriculum for their schools. It is a thorough and sometimes grueling process. However, it is necessary to select the most viable product available.

The second option that educators have is creating their own curriculum. Taking this route requires forethought as well. Just as in selecting a third-party-generated curriculum, it is best to first establish a framework for analysis—a rubric—to ensure that expectations are met. A proposed rubric is provided later in this chapter. If the organization elects to create its own digital civics and citizenship curriculum, timing is crucial. A good, workable curriculum takes time to develop, test, and revise.

Developing a curriculum requires subject matter experts. These can be identified within the local learning community. The primary challenge with recruiting subject matter experts is time. Many of the available subject matter experts may be educators as well or work in the education industry, which means that creating a curriculum will most likely be done outside of their normal work time. Each organization has to arrive at its own unique solution to this challenge as it arises.

RUBRIC

The term *rubric* was originally established in ecclesiastical use, referring to a particular liturgical tradition or practice. Over time, the term moved into more common use, especially within the realm of education. For this text, a rubric is a visual set of expectations or qualities within a curriculum that are measured on an established scale in order to rank the quality and effectiveness of the curriculum itself.

The following rubric is a starting point. It is a general framework for a group to begin discussing and thinking about adopting a digital civics and citizenship curriculum for use in its specific education context. This rubric is provided as a recommendation, and it should be adapted for use in the unique context that a group or committee may be operating in to select a curriculum. It is a tool, not a cure or a prescient prognosticator. This rubric can help guide educators in making a decision; it cannot make the decision for them.

This rubric is also helpful if the group decides to create a curriculum. Just as it provides a framework for analyzing a third-party curriculum, it can also help to evaluate a curriculum as it is generated. Better yet, educators can utilize the rubric as a framework for planning, developing, and designing the curriculum.

This rubric draws on the Wisconsin model for evaluating community education,[1] Aristotle's virtues,[2] and the cardinal and theological virtues examined by St. Thomas Aquinas.[3] While this last source may be a point of contention in the United States, where the Constitution establishes a definite separation between church and state, or in non-Christian nations, there is a solution.

The theological and cardinal virtues are easily defined and transferred into a secular perspective. For nations and communities that are religiously based and possibly religiously led, the theological understanding of these virtues transcends creeds, denominations, and beliefs. This is part of the adaptation that is required for each community to best embed digital civics and citizenship into its teaching, learning, and curriculum development practices.

The rubric provides a tool for analyzing and evaluating digital civics and citizenship curricula. It is meant to be a starting point for examining potential curricula or developing a curriculum in-house. Educators can adapt this tool as needed to address the specific context in which digital civics and citizenship are to be taught, learned, and practiced. Users should feel confident in modifying this rubric as necessary without fearing loss of fidelity.

Working with the Rubric

This rubric, like any rubric, is a tool. There are different ways to use it, and it can be modified and adapted as necessary. The rubric provides a bridge from initial discussions of *whether* digital civics and citizenship should be taught to *how* digital civics and citizenship should be taught. In a mythological

Table 14.1.   Sample Rubric

Four-Point Grading Scale	1	2	3	4
Leadership development				
Localization				
Integrated delivery of services				
Maximum use of resources				
Inclusiveness				
Responsiveness				
Lifelong learning				

sense, according to Joseph Campbell, this is the response portion of the hero's journey.[4]

Using Campbell's paradigm, this second step in the journey follows the initial call to action. Using this perspective, we can see the rise in cyberbullying, catfishing, gaslighting, and other detrimental digital deviousness as the call to action. Attempts have been made, with some success, in training counselors and public school teachers to recognize these incidents and work with students who are the victims. Yet there are few formal learning experiences that directly address not only individual online behavior but creating and cultivating positive and healthy online communities.

Users of this rubric can employ it primarily in two ways. The first is as an identification matrix. The second is as a scoring analysis when reviewing or planning a curriculum for digital civics and citizenship. In both cases, the rubric provides instructors and administrators with a focused overview of the curriculum being reviewed. This analysis works for either type of curriculum, third-party-vendor supplied or in-house generated.

Analyzing a Vendor-Supplied Curriculum

Utilizing this rubric, either in its present form or adapted, to analyze a third-party curriculum is fairly straightforward. The following steps provide the recommended process in using the rubric for analyzing a curriculum:

1. Divide each box in the matrix in half. This can be done either vertically or horizontally.
2. Go through the curriculum and identify the location where the criteria are met and record this in one half of the appropriate box.
3. Analyze how well the criteria are addressed and record this in the other half of the corresponding box.

4. Color-code the boxes: red = little or no mention of the criteria, yellow = survey exploration of the criteria, and green = full analysis of the criteria.

Once the committee has reviewed the selected curriculum, the next step is to tally up the analyses and arrive at a composite score. All of the matrices should be compiled and compared by the committee. The curriculum with the greatest amount of green is the best tool available for teaching digital civics and citizenship in the local context of the committee. Also consider other reviewed curricula with the least amount of red in the composite analysis.

Planning and Analyzing an In-House Curriculum

An organization that plans to develop and deploy its own digital civics and citizenship curriculum can utilize the rubric in three ways:

*   planning document
*   quality assurance tool
*   revision tool

Planning Document

Using the matrix as a planning document is a powerful means of leveraging this tool to outline and lay out the proposed curriculum. Once the decision is made by the committee to create a digital civics and citizenship curriculum, the undertaking can seem daunting. However, the rubric can help to identify the constituent parts needed in the curriculum. It also opens discussion among the committee, curriculum developers, instructional designers, and subject matter experts. These discussions are vital to produce the best possible product.

The rubric also provides the committee with a tool to begin outlining the proposed curriculum. Just as the rubric outlines the principles and facets of a digital civics and citizenship course by which to analyze a curriculum, it also lays out what needs to be taught, practiced, and implemented through a created curriculum. By shifting the understanding and perspective of the rubric, it becomes apparent how the same tool functions as a starting outline for creating a curriculum.

QA Tool

Utilizing the rubric as a quality assurance (QA) tool during and after development works in a similar way. For quality assurance, the rubric provides a means of assessing the curriculum as it is produced, as well as for evaluating the completed product. Just as the rubric is used to identify the what, where, and how of a third-party curriculum, it can be used in the same way for quality assurance checks on a curriculum generated in-house. The recommended use for the rubric as a QA tool hinges on answering the following questions:

1. Where in the curriculum is the particular skill or piece of knowledge introduced, explained, practiced, and assessed?
2. How is the skill or knowledge introduced, explained, practiced, and assessed?
3. To what depth and complexity is the skill or knowledge introduced, explained, practiced, and assessed?

The data collected using this QA tool is invaluable. It provides information crucial to creating an authentic and engaging digital civics and citizenship curriculum. Similarly, this data is the foundation for the third use of the rubric, as a revision tool.

Revision Tool

When an organization decides to incorporate the recommended rubric as a revision tool for digital civics and citizenship education, the matrix can function in a very similar way to its use as a tool for planning and organization, development, or analysis. The rubric provides a useful tool for analyzing, revising, and updating an existing curriculum currently being utilized.

The matrix allows users to identify gaps in knowledge and skills. Similarly, it reveals areas where knowledge or skills need to be updated. Using the same red, yellow, and green classification scale described earlier in the chapter makes it possible to triage the curriculum and makes it easier to organize a revision plan. The following analysis scale is recommended when using the rubric for revision work:

red = immediate revision
yellow = revision as time allows
green = no revision needed

Of course this is a simplified understanding of using the rubric as a revision tool for a reason. This initial basic approach provides greater opportunity for organizations that adopt this tool and adapt it to their specific needs. As a result, the tool is more transferrable and translatable across a greater variety of contexts and situations. This adaptability also adds longevity to usage of the tool.

INSTRUCTIONAL DEVELOPMENT

The best curriculum in the world is absolutely worthless without an equal caliber of instruction to communicate it to learners. In fact, the best curriculum without instruction would only be effective as a doorstop in most cases. Unlike other content areas, digital civics and citizenship is not a course or class for which any educator could simply review the scope and sequence of the curriculum and be successful at teaching. Just as selecting or generating a curriculum for digital civics and citizenship is an involved process, preparing educators to teach it demands a certain amount of training and preparation.

The topic of faculty and staff buy-in regarding implementing digital civics and citizenship will be explained later. Buy-in is a crucial aspect of successfully teaching and learning digital civics and citizenship in an organization. However, adding relevancy as well as rigor to the curriculum selected or created not only assists in strengthening faculty and staff buy-in regarding digital civics and citizenship but also guides learners in recognizing and appreciating the embeddedness of this particular body of knowledge and skills in everyday life.

One of the earliest and surest means of instructional development with digital civics and citizenship is having grade-level teams in K–12, departments in higher education, and colleagues in community education conduct what is referred to as a crosswalk of learning objectives, standards, or outcomes with their content and the new material. This undertaking is literally placing the digital civics and citizenship curriculum side-by-side with the curriculum taught in other departments, courses, and workshops. Working with a transdisciplinary team allows instructors to collaborate in finding intersecting and parallel areas within the different curricula. Doing this reveals times and places where instructors can guide students across disciplines and content areas.

Learning and practicing new knowledge and skills in this manner provides not only a more holistic dimension to the learning experience but also a more realistic hue. Outside of traditional learning environments, most knowledge and skills are gained experientially and holistically. Rarely is something taught in a vacuum. Individuals acquire these new skills and bodies of knowledge within the relational context of a larger life experience.

One of the lasting results of this is that the particular skill or piece of knowledge is tied to an emotional memory from the overall experience. This fact about learning can help to transition the newly acquired knowledge and skill in the learner's mind from short-term to long-term memory. Care must be taken in order to ensure that the emotions binding the pieces of knowledge and skills to the memory are mostly positive. This does not mean that learners should not be challenged. Instructors, however, must be attuned to the effective and productive level of frustration for each learner to make the acquisition a rewarding experience. These levels of frustration vary from learner to learner. As such, it is incumbent upon the instructor to know their students.

While this aspect is not necessarily new to teaching and learning, it does help to instigate as well as to fortify the successful implementation of a stand-alone digital civics and citizenship course within an established learning environment. With this understanding, the necessity of integrating digital civics and citizenship teaching and learning into the established curriculum becomes evident. Conducting a curriculum crosswalk is the surest way of providing relevance and fidelity in this integration.

This chapter has explored the approach of having a stand-alone digital civics and citizenship course or learning experience. It examined the options of utilizing a third-party curriculum or developing an in-house curriculum. Finally, it provided a rubric for curriculum analysis, creation, and revision. The rubric's uses were explored, and recommended approaches were provided.

Perhaps the greatest takeaway from this chapter is the commitment needed for teaching and learning digital civics and citizenship from an operations and administrative perspective. Education administrators must allot time and resources to the individuals or groups that will be instructing and sometimes creating or revising the curriculum. Learning is a long-term commitment and process for teachers as well as learners. This understanding carried throughout the process helps to guarantee the overall success of everyone involved.

NOTES

1. The community education principles were developed by Larry Horyna and Larry Decker for the National Coalition for Community Education (1991).
2. J. E. C. Welldon, trans. and ed., *The Nicomachean Ethics of Aristotle, with Critical Analysis* (London: Macmillan, 1897).
3. St. Thomas Aquinas, *Summa Theologica* (London: Burns, 1922).
4. Joseph Campbell, *The Hero with a Thousand Faces* (Princeton, NJ: Princeton University Press, 2004).

Chapter Fifteen

Sample Lesson Plans and Learning Activities

LESSON #1: DEFINING WHAT WE KNOW

Guiding Question: What does digital civics and citizenship look like at _____? (insert the name of school or organization)

Engage: (Analog) Fold a piece of paper into equal thirds. Turn the paper landscape. Draw lines on the two folds. Label the top of each column with one of the following: Digital, Civics, and Citizenship. Learners will create an icon representing their understanding of each. (Digital) Have students open a new presentation using a tool such as PowerPoint. Learners will create three slides. Each one is to be labeled with one of the following: Digital, Civics, and Citizenship. Learners will create an icon representing their understanding of each.

Explore: Learners will share results with the group and have a whole-group discussion.[1]

Explain: The facilitator/instructor will provide the group with dictionary definitions of the terms.

Elaborate: Learners will compare and contrast their created icons and explanations with the dictionary definitions as a whole group.

Evaluate: Under the guidance of the instructor, learners will generate new icons and definitions from their comparing and contrasting efforts to generate unified icons and definitions of the terms "Digital," "Civics," and "Citizenship," reporting their findings in a digital presentation, an infographic, or a poster to share with the larger community.

LESSON #2: DIGITAL RIGHTS AND RESPONSIBILITIES

Guiding Question: As a digital citizen, what are my responsibilities and rights within the digital community?

Engage: Learners will read and review information from the following sites:

- https://www.digitalcitizenship.net/nine-elements.html
- https://www.coe.int/en/web/digital-citizenship-education/rights-and-responsibilities
- http://fw-d7-freedomworks-org.s3.amazonaws.com/FreedomWorks%20Digital%20Bill%20of%20Rights.pdf

Learners will collaborate with each other and create what they believe is a Digital Bill of Rights for their community.

Explore: Under the guidance of the instructor, learners will review the information on the following sites:

- https://www.archives.gov/founding-docs/bill-of-rights-transcript
- https://www.un.org/en/universal-declaration-human-rights

Learners will compare and contrast their Digital Bill of Rights with these two documents.

Explain: Under the guidance of the instructor, learners will explore and answer the following questions:

- What is a Digital Bill of Rights?
- What needs to be included in a Digital Bill of Rights?
- Why is a Digital Bill of Rights necessary?
- Who is responsible for a Digital Bill of Rights?
- How is a Digital Bill of Rights safeguarded and enforced?

Elaborate: Under the guidance of the instructor, learners will begin drafting a Digital Bill of Rights for use in their community.

Evaluate: With the assistance of the instructor, learners will generate a Digital Bill of Rights for display and use in their community. (Medium: group's choice.)

LESSON #3: ACTA ET VERSA

Guiding Question: What does digital citizenship and civics look like in daily interactions?

Engage: Students will generate individual lists of words, phrases, and acts that reflect best practices of digital citizenship and civics. (Medium: instructor's choice.)

Explore: Under the guidance of the instructor, learners will share their lists, compare and contrast them, and discuss/debate their importance and relevance in the digital world.

Explain: Through an instructor-led discussion, learners will use the following sites to discuss the civic actions and language used by digital citizens:

- https://couragetocare.org.au
- https://www.brookings.edu/blog/education-plus-development/2019/11/12/the-bucket-list-for-involved-citizens-76-things-you-can-do-to-boost-civic-engagement
- https://www.learningtogive.org/resources/civic-responsibility

Elaborate: Under the guidance of the instructor, students will compare and contrast their lists with the information provided by the listed websites, as well as any sites selected by the instructor or identified by the learners.

Evaluate: In group collaboration, students will generate an infographic listing some of the more popular and recognized civic actions and language that digital citizens can utilize daily. (Medium: instructor/learner choice.)

LESSON #4: CIVITAS AND COMMUNITAS

Guiding Question: How can digital citizens share their knowledge and skills to cultivate digital civics and citizenship in their respective communities?

Engage: Students will examine current offerings and resources for digital civics and citizenship education and practice. The following sites are good starting points:

- http://digitalcivics.org/about
- https://digitalcivics.io
- https://www.coe.int/en/web/digital-citizenship-education/digital-citizenship-and-digital-citizenship-education

Learners will record what efforts are in existence to educate and encourage individuals to practice digital civics and citizenship.

Explore: Facilitated by the instructor, learners will share their findings. A single "report" will be generated to work from in the subsequent parts of this learning experience. (Medium: learner/instructor choice.)

Explain: Instructor-led exploration of the pros and cons of these offerings. Compare and contrast these offerings and resources with what is available within the local community. Create a collaborative reporting instrument. (Medium: learner choice.)

Elaborate: Learner-led analysis of the "gaps" in both the local and larger offerings for digital civics and citizenship education and practice. Learners will add to the existing reporting instrument with their findings. Collaboratively brainstorm recommended solutions to advocate for locally.

Evaluate: Learner-generated communication with local agencies and organizations for creating and implementing recommended changes to current digital civics and citizenship education and practice opportunities. With instructor guidance, learners will identify individuals within the organizations and agencies to address these recommendations to and send them.

LESSON #5: IGNORANCE IS THE BEGINNING OF ALL WISDOM

Guiding Question: What can digital citizens do to help the practice of digital civics and citizenship continue to grow and evolve over time in their respective communities?

Engage: Using the format from the "Engage" portion of lesson 1, learners will title their slides or columns "18 months," "3 years," and "5 years." In each column, learners will further divide each column into "Digital Community" and "Geographic Community" sections. In each of these sections, learners will identify actions they will take to further their knowledge and practice of digital civics and citizenship, as well as to further it in their respective communities. (Medium: learner choice.)

Explore: Instructor-guided sharing from students. The whole group will collaboratively report their findings. (Medium: instructor choice.) The whole group will compare and contrast their shared ideas to select two to three actions to list on the shared reporting instrument.

Explain: Instructor-guided analysis of the selected actions. The focus of the analysis will be to scrutinize each one for feasibility and sustainability in their respective contexts. The instructor will play the role of devil's advocate.

Elaborate: Learner-led collaboration of selecting one action for each "community" and in each column. As a whole group, learners will answer the following questions:

- What will this action look like?
- How will success be measured?
- When will practice of this action begin?
- Who will this action be directed toward? Who is the intended audience?
- Where will evidence of this action be found?

- To what extent will this action be adaptable?

Evaluate: Learner-led collaboration to generate a group contract implementing the information and actions arrived at in the previous steps of this learning experience. Learners will be encouraged to affix their signatures to this contract, creating a reflective and responsible community whose members will help hold one another responsible for their actions regarding digital civics and citizenship.

LEARNING PLAN #1: RETHINKING AND RETOOLING THE "COMPLIMENT SANDWICH" FOR DIGITAL CIVICS AND CITIZENSHIP

In the professional realm, the communication tool referred to as the "compliment sandwich"[2] was misused and overused. As a result, it has now become a cautionary phrase with regard to leadership, communication, and team building. However, utilized in a truer form, it can be a powerful tool for practicing digital civics and citizenship.

This will be explored momentarily. For now, the question of what a compliment sandwich is needs to be answered. A compliment sandwich is a communication construct that is utilized to provide a corrective statement sandwiched between two compliments. It looks something like this:

TEAM LEAD: "Good morning. How're you doing today?"

TEAM MEMBER: "Good, thanks."

TEAM LEAD: "Good work on the project. It's really shaping up to be a winner."

TEAM MEMBER: "Thanks. I appreciate you noticing."

TEAM LEAD: "Sure. I've also noticed that it seems like something is keeping you from getting into the office on time lately."

TEAM MEMBER: "Yeah. Sorry about that. I'll try harder to make sure I get in on time."

TEAM LEAD: "Let's grab a cup of coffee and see if we can figure something out. I want to help. Sometimes having a different set of eyes to look at the situation makes the difference."

TEAM MEMBER: "Oh, okay."

Many management specialists and leadership coaches have noted that too often the compliment sandwich falls short of achieving its goal. Some even report that it results in compliments being taken as disingenuous and associating negative experiences with them. Part of the challenge is making sure the compliment aligns with the critique. In other words, a compliment sandwich is too often served in this manner:

TEAM LEAD: "Good morning. Hey, nice shoes!"

TEAM MEMBER: "Oh. Thank you."

TEAM LEAD: "Listen, I need you to make it in on time. This is your verbal warning."

TEAM MEMBER: "Oh . . . uh . . . I apologize, but I'm . . ."

TEAM LEAD: "Have a nice day. See you tomorrow . . . on time."

In the digital realm, verbal communication is even trickier since individuals cannot always see others' facial expressions and body language. Words and phrases often take on new meanings with the receiver. With this in mind, digital citizens can retool the compliment sandwich and effectively use it in an online conversation. For instance, the scenario might look something like this:

PERSON A: "I think Prop 221B is stupid and a waste of taxpayers' money!"

PERSON B: "Interesting. I appreciate your directness on the topic. Would you like to share why you think that?"

PERSON A: "Duh! Like I said, it's stupid and a waste!"

PERSON B: "Okay. What specifically do you think is stupid about it?"

PERSON A: "Wow! Are you really that stupid that you want to waste taxpayers' money?"

PERSON B: "Well, I don't agree that it's a waste per se. Also, please don't call me stupid. I'd like to understand your perspective better. Would you please explain further?"

PERSON A: "Whatever."

While this is not necessarily an ideal exchange, it is representative of what commonly occurs online, especially when subjects like politics and religion are being discussed. Learning and practicing the skill of the compliment sandwich works best in scenario-based learning exercises. It is recommended that these exercises be implemented with a two-phased approach. Recommended implementation would look something like this:

> Phase 1: Instructor leads the exercise in the role of the other individual in the exchange.
> Phase 2: Learners are paired up and take turns in the roles.

LESSON PLAN #2: STYLIZING DIGITAL CIVICS AND CITIZENSHIP

It's no surprise that learners are growing more visually literate and conversant as a result of ubiquitous advances in technology, especially in social media. Emojis and memes are regular constituents of daily communication. Icons have replaced titles on computer screens. In fact, it is very difficult for almost anyone to navigate their home screen or a website without some general knowledge of icons. Ironically, most learners cannot identify when they acquired the knowledge of what the different icons mean. Within the realm of social media, the meanings of some icons change daily, if not more often.

With part of the focus of digital civics and citizenship instruction and practice being communication, leveraging these three tools can be efficacious in the digital realm. Rather than struggling against the use of emojis, icons, and memes, digital civics and citizenship instructors can leverage the power and ubiquity of these things in the digital realm to help learners practice their newfound knowledge and skills. Creating and utilizing these communication tools can empower learners not only in communicating but also in building and strengthening digital communities.

When learners and practitioners create and utilize digital civics and citizenship emojis, icons, and memes, it assists in creating a sense of both ownership and community with each individual. As a result, individuals experience a sense of responsibility at varying levels. This assists in creating and cultivating a digital community that is civil in nature.

The following lesson provides a framework for instruction and practicing the collaborative creation and utilization of emojis, icons, and memes for digital civics and citizenship. As with the other recommendations found in this text, this learning experience should be adapted to the context and audience for which it is being used.

Part 1: Show Me What You're Saying

Guiding Question: Why are emojis, icons, and memes so popular?

Engage: Students will identify their favorite emoji, icon, and meme (one each) that is appropriate for the situation. Learners will collect their choices for sharing with the group. (Medium: instructor choice.)

Explore: Students will share their selections, explaining what message these communicate and why they selected these pieces.

Explain: Under the guidance of the instructor, the group will create working definitions of the following terms:

- emoji
- icon
- meme

Elaborate: Instructor will share "why" these three tools of communication work. The following sites will help to explain:

Emojis   https://www.forbes.com/sites/bryanrobinson/2019/09/07/emojis-an-essential-tool-for-innovative-business-communication-really/?sh=3c475b6bc9e6

Icons   https://www.inc.com/alison-davis/need-a-quick-way-to-communicate-try-an-icon.html

Memes   https://strategicsocialmedialab.com/the-power-of-memes-in-social-media-communication

Evaluate: Utilizing the newly acquired knowledge regarding emojis, icons, and memes, students will add to their reporting tool two or three sentences explaining why these things are powerful communication tools, as well as their meaning.

Part 2: Show Me, Don't Tell Me

Guiding Question: How can an individual visually communicate the philosophy and practices of digital civics and citizenship?

Engage: Students will research and identify existing emojis, icons, and memes that can be used in practicing digital civics and citizenship. (Medium: instructor choice.)

Explore: Students will share their findings with the whole group, explaining the meaning of each. (If students have gaps in their reporting or cannot find any, hold until the next step.)

Explain: Lead with these questions for whole-group discussion:

- Why do you think these emojis, icons, and memes were created?

- What other emojis, icons, and memes are needed for digital civics and citizenship?

Elaborate: Each student creates an emoji, icon, or meme of their choosing to share with the whole group. (Add to existing reporting tool.)

Evaluate: Students will share their creation but not the message they are attempting to communicate. Other students will attempt to identify the message. The whole group will collaborate on any recommended revisions or changes to the emojis, icons, or memes shared. These are not to be made yet.

Part 3: Go Forth and Multiply

Guiding Question: How can you create and apply new emojis, icons, and memes in the practice of digital civics and citizenship?

Engage: Students will revise the emojis, icons, and memes from the previous portion of the learning experience. Use the reporting tool from part 2.

Explore: Students will share their revisions and changes with the whole group. The group will critique in regard to clarity of communication and understanding. (The instructor can use a Likert scale for the judgments.)

Explain: Under the guidance of the instructor, the whole group will identify why these revisions and changes were necessary. The instructor will maintain the focus on the universality of the message being communicated through the emoji, icon, or meme.

Elaborate: Students will create an emoji, icon, and meme needed for identified practices of digital civics and citizenship, especially communication. The following is a list of some suggested practices:

- civil discourse
- ethical treatment of others
- respectful disagreement
- rule of law
- community standards
- inalienable rights
- individual liberties

Evaluate: As in part 2, students will share their creations, explaining how they will be used in the digital realm, and the whole group will attempt to identify the practice as well as to critique the emoji's, icon's, and meme's effectiveness.

NOTES

1. https://sites.nationalacademies.org/cs/groups/dbassesite/documents/webpage/dbasse_073327.pdf.

2. https://www.leadershipiq.com/blogs/leadershipiq/compliment-sandwich.

Chapter Sixteen

Standards, Outcomes, and Objectives

In the past few decades, learning standards have become a greater determining factor of what is taught in K–12 education in the United States. Standards are a highly contested topic within the realm of public education, with little or no hint of cooling down anytime in the near future. However, the establishment and use of standards in teaching and learning is actually quite useful for all involved. This is no different for digital civics and citizenship. Regardless of the context in which these subjects are taught, having learning standards, outcomes, and objectives clearly identified and articulated helps guide learners and teachers through the content successfully.

These terms—learning *standards*, *outcomes*, and *objectives*—are often misused as interchangeable by many individuals. This stems from a misunderstanding of the subtle nuances and shades of difference in meaning between these three educational terms. Therefore, this chapter will identify, define, and differentiate learning standards, outcomes, and objectives.

LEARNING STANDARDS

Learning standards are the measurements by which teachers and students are assessed in the United States within the K–12 spectrum. These standards identify *what* is to be learned by the students at a particular grade level and within a particular content area. They also identify *how* the mastery of knowledge or a skill is to be measured. This is founded upon Bloom's taxonomy.[1] The standards for a subject as a whole also help to provide a scope and sequence, addressing *when* the knowledge or skill will be taught. The *where* is understood as in the classroom, whatever context that may be. The *who* is understood as the students who learn the material.

This leaves the *why* to be answered. The question of *why?* is always a difficult one for educators to address, and even more challenging for students to answer. Most commonly students are informed that they need to learn the particular knowledge or skill because it's in the standards, or because it will be on the state assessment. Needless to say, these are two of the worst answers that can be given when trying to ascertain why something should be learned. For a more thorough examination regarding the question of *why?* please see Simon Sinek's seminal work on engaging individuals by understanding their "why."[2]

For the purposes of this work, the term *standards* is understood as follows:

> Identified learning pieces focused on one skill or piece of knowledge, with the focus being on the depth of mastery a learner needs to obtain through practice, measured using Bloom's taxonomy.[3]

With this definition of learning standards, the question of their importance naturally follows, especially in regard to digital civics and citizenship. Simply put, learning standards clearly articulate what a course at a particular level will cover in regard to content knowledge and skills. They also identify the depth of rigor students can expect when working to master that piece of knowledge or skill.

Having learning standards provide this information guides instructors in creating learning experiences that introduce and work with the piece of knowledge or skill, as well as in assessing their mastery. Similarly, learning standards assist instructors, curriculum developers, and instructional designers in creating appropriate practices and assessments for learners. This type of approach to teaching and learning is often referred to as *scaffolding* in education.[4] Scaffolding provides learners with the opportunity to master new knowledge and skills built upon the foundation of those already mastered. This approach is crucial in developing lifelong learning practice in learners.

Within many of the accepted state and federal learning standards currently used in the United States, there are components of civics and citizenship education embedded either implicitly or explicitly. Similarly, there are well-defined technology-focused learning standards. However, a codified body of learning standards for digital civics and citizenship does not exist.

One of the best starting places for generating learning standards explicitly for digital civics and citizenship is with existing learning standards. The National Council for the Social Studies (NCSS) created a set of learning standards for K–12 education known as the College, Career, and Civic Life Framework for Social Studies State Standards (C3).[5] Given the fact that these standards are focused on social studies, building upon them for digital civics and citizenship is not difficult. The following is an example:

D2.Civ.7.K–2. Apply civic virtues when participating in school settings.

D2.Civ.7.3–5. Apply civic virtues and democratic principles in school settings.

D2.Civ.7.6–8. Apply civic virtues and democratic principles in school and community settings.

D2.Civ.7.9–12. Apply civic virtues and democratic principles when working with others.

D2.Civ.8.K–2. Describe democratic principles such as equality, fairness, and respect for legitimate authority and rules.

D2.Civ.8.3–5. Identify core civic virtues and democratic principles that guide government, society, and communities.

D2.Civ.8.6–8. Analyze ideas and principles contained in the founding documents of the United States, and explain how they influence the social and political system.

D2.Civ.8.9–12. Evaluate social and political systems in different contexts, times, and places that promote civic virtues and enact democratic principles.

D2.Civ.9.K–2. Follow agreed-upon rules for discussions while responding attentively to others when addressing ideas and making decisions as a group.

D2.Civ.9.3–5. Use deliberative processes when making decisions or reaching judgments as a group.

D2.Civ.9.6–8. Compare deliberative processes used by a wide variety of groups in various settings.

D2.Civ.9.9–12. Use appropriate deliberative processes in multiple settings.

D2.Civ.10.K–2. Compare their own point of view with others' perspectives.

D2.Civ.10.3–5. Identify the beliefs, experiences, perspectives, and values that underlie their own and others' points of view about civic issues.

D2.Civ.10.6–8. Explain the relevance of personal interests and perspectives, civic virtues, and democratic principles when people address issues and problems in constitutional rights and human rights.

D2.Civ.10.9–12. Analyze the impact and the appropriate roles of personal interests and perspectives on the application of civic virtues, democratic principles, government, and civil society.

SUGGESTED K–12 PATHWAY FOR COLLEGE, CAREER, AND CIVIC READINESS, DIMENSION 2: PARTICIPATION AND DELIBERATION

This table, taken from the NCSS publication *College, Career and Civic Life C3 Framework for Social Studies State Standards*, spans the learning experience from kindergarten through high school. By inserting words and phrases such as *digitally*, *online*, *using social media*, and *on discussion boards* at the end of the majority of these standards translates them easily for use in digital civics and citizenship education.

This is true for the realms of higher and community education. By continuing these standards further into the adult spectrum, adapting these learning standards is easier than starting from scratch. The primary objection to developing and using learning standards in higher and community education is that these areas of teaching and learning are different from K–12 education. This is true. However, good pedagogy and good teaching translate across the life spectrum of learners.

With this in mind, for higher and community education, instead of focusing on learning standards it is recommended that educators at these levels look at outcomes first. Learning outcomes are explored in the next section. As will become evident, learning outcomes and standards work hand-in-hand when developing and designing learning experiences, regardless of the audience.

LEARNING OUTCOMES

Learning outcomes are simply goals. These goals are shared by both the learners and the instructors in a learning experience. Most often, learning outcomes are encountered within higher education, professional development, and community education. There are good reasons that outcomes are more at home in these realms than they would be in the K–12 educational spectrum.

First of all, in adult education, including the area of higher education, participants are focused on what they are going to get out of their efforts and expense. This is increasingly true given the high cost of a college or university education. The same holds true for professional development and community education. In these areas, participants are working adults with responsibilities other than education, such as work and family. As such, their time is limited. Participants want a sort of guarantee for the expenditure of their time and money.

Learning outcomes provide this to a certain extent. They are something like an agreement between the instructor and participants. They can be understood as an agreed-upon contract between two parties. Instructors are guaranteeing that participants will be exposed to and will practice certain skills and pieces of knowledge. This is in return for participants' agreement to provide the instructor with their time and participation. In an economic sense, learning outcomes facilitate an exchange.

For digital civics and citizenship education, learning outcomes are a powerful tool not only for attracting participants but also for securing funding and additional support. These last two aspects are crucial pieces for overall success in professional development and community education. These areas of teaching and learning are definitely driven by budgetary and administrative support for success and longevity.

Here are some examples of learning outcomes for digital civics and citizenship education created for the purposes of this text.

By completing this learning experience, participants will be able to do the following:

- Explain what digital civics and citizenship is.
- Identify best practices for digital civics and citizenship.
- Apply digital civics and citizenship practices to different scenarios.
- Analyze sample social media posts for evidence of digital civics and citizenship.
- Evaluate the effectiveness of practicing digital civics and citizenship in daily exchanges on social media.
- Create expanded individual perspectives and understandings of being an engaged global citizen using digital civics and citizenship.

These are just examples. Yet they can be easily lifted from this text and placed into any learning experience for digital civics and citizenship. Similarly, these sample learning outcomes follow the progressive complexity and rigor found in Bloom's taxonomy. Learning outcomes are also a useful tool in designing and developing the learning experience. This process of working backward in a sense has already been examined in a previous chapter concerning stand-alone digital civics and citizenship courses.

Learning outcomes are similar to learning standards but have an important difference. One way to keep this difference clear is to think of learning outcomes as guarantees to participants from the instructor, while learning standards are expectations of what learners should strive to master. Although both are firmly rooted in teaching and learning, the approach and understanding to teaching and learning are markedly different.

LEARNING OBJECTIVES

Learning objectives also are similar to learning standards and learning outcomes. In fact, in most traditional educational settings, learning objectives are constructed using the other two components. As with the other two parts of educational pedagogy, the term *learning objectives* is sometimes misused as a synonym for learning standards or learning outcomes. Just as those two are similar yet have marked differences, so too do learning objectives.

Learning objectives are akin to a participant-focused version of learning standards. Whereas learning standards anticipate educators as their audience and use educational jargon, learning objectives are aimed at learners and use more common speech in their construction. In other words, when participants in a course are asked what they are learning, they are able to answer using learning objectives. More than just an exercise in rote memorization, learning objectives provide students with the ability to not just recite what they are learning or practicing but to authentically communicate the knowledge or skill they are working with. Analyzing learning objectives from an economic perspective, we can understand these facets of teaching and learning as an exchange. When individuals give their time and attention to a student in asking them what they are doing, the student can provide the answer using a learning objective. The objective provides students with a tool to communicate with others, as well as understanding what it is they are learning and practicing.

For use in digital civics and citizenship learning experiences, instructors can take information from learning standards to craft learning objectives. Here is an example of how this might be done. The following learning standards are taken from the NCSS C3 standards[6] presented earlier in this chapter:

D2.Civ.9.K–2. Follow agreed-upon rules for discussions while responding attentively to others when addressing ideas and making decisions as a group.

D2.Civ.9.3–5. Use deliberative processes when making decisions or reaching judgments as a group.

D2.Civ.9.6–8. Compare deliberative processes used by a wide variety of groups in various settings.

D2.Civ.9.9–12. Use appropriate deliberative processes in multiple settings.

The learning objectives that can be generated from these standards could include these:

- Conduct and participate in a civil discussion using agreed-upon rules.
- Deliberate as a group to arrive at a shared decision or judgment.

- Compare and contrast how different groups arrive at a shared decision.
- Apply different processes in a variety of settings to arrive at a shared decision.

If you compare the learning objectives with the learning standards, you will notice many similarities. What these two sets of information are used to address does not change. The two primary differences are *how* the knowledge or skill is addressed and *who* the intended audience is. Basically, the difference is language. But we must be careful with language. Language is the foundation of digital civics and citizenship and must be wielded as precisely as possible.

It is recommended that digital civics and citizenship educators practice and experiment generating learning objectives. As shown, the recommended practice of doing this is straightforward. The key is focusing on appropriate language for the intended audience. Educators should use language that the learners would use in their regular communications with peers and others. By being able to communicate with others what they are learning, students begin to take control of their own learning and deepen their comprehension of what they are learning.

WRITING LEARNING OBJECTIVES, STANDARDS, AND OUTCOMES

From the above examination of these three pedagogical tools, there are some commonalities that all three share. For many veteran educators at every level, generating a feasible learning standard, outcome, or objective can seem almost impossible. In fact, some educators refer to these pieces of instruction as magic. They do not know where these pieces come from, how they are made, or who makes them. Yet there is something of a formula that can be employed when having to generate proprietary learning standards, objectives, and outcomes.

Like a SMART goal,[7] these learning pieces have definite and required components. Essentially these facets answer the simple questions of *who*, *what*, *how*, and *to what extent*. In other words, a well-constructed learning standard will be able to supply the following information:

- Who is learning?
- What are they learning?
- How will they learn, practice, and be assessed on this learning?
- To what extent (read: depth) will they learn this knowledge/skill?

As discussed in a previous chapter, the *when* is addressed in the curriculum and instructional scope and sequence. The only other question left to answer is the *why*. This is the eternal question. For digital civics and citizenship, the entire journey of learning and practicing the knowledge and skills contained within the curriculum addresses this question. At the heart of it, digital civics and citizenship helps individuals frame their answers to the questions, "Why should I be a good citizen online?" "What is my civic responsibility and duty online?" and "How am I a citizen online?"

With this understanding in mind, generating a single learning objective, outcome, or standard for digital civics and citizenship can be understood as helping learners to construct their answers to these questions. For example, the question, "Why should I be a good citizen online?" can be partially addressed by the following standard:

> The learner will analyze a situation of cyberbullying and identify how this situation could be best handled, and if possible avoided, while ensuring that all parties involved can exercise their human rights by providing possible alternatives to cyberbullying.

Review the first set of questions regarding generating learning standards, objectives, and outcomes. Does this standard answer the questions as fully as possible? Does it provide a modicum of flexibility for a diversity of learning styles in a variety of contexts? Where might improvements be made in this learning standard?

While the answer to the first two questions is a yes, a rejoinder of "to some extent" must be added. No learning standard is perfect. Nor does any single learning standard, objective, or outcome completely address all that a student must master in a single learning experience. However, the above learning standard is workable. Its deficiencies can be remedied within the learning environment by the instructor.

When constructing a learning standard, outcome, or objective, the following formula, for lack of a better term, is useful for getting started:

Who? + What? + How? + To what extent? = Learning standard, outcome, objective

As with any recommendation and guidance provided in this text, this formula is not the be-all and end-all in regard to generating learning standards, outcomes, or objectives in digital civics and citizenship. It's a starting point—nothing more, nothing less. It should be treated as such.

Adaptations and improvements are not merely solicited but demanded in order that the learning standards, outcomes, and objectives are transferrable, scalable, and adaptable for as wide a variety of learning contexts and audiences as possible.

Learning standards, outcomes, and objectives are crucial parts of teaching and learning and powerful tools in curriculum development and instructional design. Standards, outcomes, and objectives vary in degree of formality. In some contexts, they are understood or unwritten. Nevertheless, they are present in some fashion in all learning experiences.

The use of standards, outcomes, and objectives in digital civics and citizenship education helps learners understand and practice the knowledge and skills presented to them in the learning experience. Similarly, these three tools assist in developing and designing learning experiences in an organized and focused manner. They help to make sense of the content.

In this chapter, we've explored some existing standards applicable to digital civics and citizenship for instructional use. Even though the existing standards are focused on K–12 learners, they can be easily translated for use in higher and community education programs. Similarly, the transition between standards, outcomes, and objectives pivots based on the audience. The intended audience determines the language to be used. With a little tinkering and experimentation, educators at all levels and working with a diversity of learners can generate standards, outcomes, and objectives for their digital civics and citizenship learning experiences. As with anything, practice is essential.

NOTES

1. Howard Gardner, *Frames of Mind: The Theory of Multiple Intelligences* (New York: Basic Books, 2011).

2. Simon Sinek, *Start with Why: How Great Leaders Inspire Everyone to Take Action* (London: Portfolio/Penguin, 2011).

3. https://cft.vanderbilt.edu/guides-sub-pages/blooms-taxonomy.

4. National Research Council, *How People Learn: Brain, Mind, Experience, and School*, expanded ed. (Washington, DC: National Academies Press, 2000).

5. https://www.socialstudies.org/c3.

6. Ibid.

7. https://www.mindtools.com/pages/article/smart-goals.htm.

Part Three

Products

Chapter Seventeen

Products and Assessments

More and more these days the measure of a "good" education is the tangible outcomes it produces in students. These can range anywhere from grades and grade point average to portfolios and projects. The increasing focus on outcome-based education has its fair share of supporters and detractors.[1] In fact, it is a universal truth that processes and programs are effectively judged by their products. The same goes for education. Regardless of the debates, schools, programs, and other educational initiatives are measured by their outcomes. This chapter examines recommended products and assessments for digital civics and citizenship education.

Two facets of teaching and learning are explored: products and assessments. These two terms are sometimes misused as synonyms. To clear up this misunderstanding, let's define *products* and *assessments* for our purposes in digital civics and citizenship education.

PRODUCTS

When someone remarks that a person is the product of their upbringing, this is the definition that is being used here. Similarly, learners are products of their experiences in schools and educational programs of every stripe. Name recognition of certain colleges and universities, such as Harvard, Princeton, and Yale, are all based on their products—that is, their successful graduates. It is these products that keep recognition and applications at consistently high levels.

For digital civics and citizenship, this understanding is secondary. *Products* in this understanding are created pieces generated by students, in addition to the students themselves. Products are a means of measuring the competency and mastery of the digital civics and citizenship knowledge and

skills learners possess. A misunderstanding that commonly occurs is referring to a test, or an assessment, as a product.

Products are more holistic in scope than assessments. While products may
focus on a particular piece of knowledge or a certain skill, they incorporate
other pieces of knowledge and skills from the learner. For example, a digital
portfolio with work examples, projects, and other components is considered a
product. With this perspective, it becomes evident that a product displays not
only a learner's competency and comprehension of the knowledge and skills,
in our case digital civics and citizenship, but also other important skills such
as design, research, writing, and other communication competencies.

Another way of understanding products is that these pieces answer the
question *what*. Products help to answer not only "What did you learn?" but
also "What can you do with this set of knowledge and skills?" Essentially,
products occupy the analysis and creation levels of Bloom's taxonomy.[2] As
such, products are complex. They both embody and display greater levels of
rigor and complexity than assessments can due to the very nature of products.
However, this does not mean that products are necessarily better as a measurement than assessments. In the next section, assessments are defined and
identified according to their usage within digital civics and citizenship. This
is followed by a comparison and differentiation of products and assessments
to better understand their relative merits.

ASSESSMENTS

As with most aspects of teaching and learning, assessments come in more
than one variety. In fact, there are seven distinct types of assessments. For the
purposes of digital civics and citizenship, this chapter explores the three most
used: diagnostic assessment, formative assessment, and summative assessment. Within all of these types, an additional "flavor" can be added with
what is referred to as an alternative assessment. For our use, the following
definitions apply to these terms.

Diagnostic assessment. Measurement used at the beginning of a learning
experience to analyze students' prior knowledge of the content. Data from
this assessment helps to identify strengths and gaps in the learners' knowledge, thus helping the teacher identify how and where to start the learning
experience to promote mastery.

Formative assessment. Measurement used during the learning and practicing of knowledge or skills to analyze student comprehension and progression. The data from these assessments help all individuals involved adjust the
teaching and learning to promote mastery.

Summative assessment. Measurement used at the completion of a learning
experience to analyze learners' mastery of the content. Data from this assess-

ment identifies where knowledge gaps are and where reteaching may be needed.

Alternative assessment. This type of assessment can augment any of the three mentioned above. This measurement instrument can take a variety of forms that are not traditional genres of assessment such as multiple choice, true/false, matching, or any other type of commonly seen questions. The data collected from this measurement provides teachers and learners the ability to analyze levels of mastery in a more applied manner.

Educators most often use the term *assessment* in reference to traditional tests and exams. Through these, students must show the level of mastery they have attained in the knowledge and skills they have learned and practiced during a certain period. Likewise, these pieces measure the impact and efficacy of the teacher's actions and planned learning experiences in imparting the desired knowledge and skills. Assessments encompass the tests and exams that are the defining measurements of both students and teachers.

This understanding sounds harsh because it is, but unnecessarily so. This pragmatic understanding is something of our own making. Rooted in traditional educational practices, neither good nor bad, assessments have attained an air of finality. In some cases, they are absolutely necessary. When the knowledge and skills are clearly measurable in an objective manner, an assessment is the best tool to use in measuring mastery. For the purposes of digital civics and citizenship, assessments are necessary. However, assessments are not the sole measurement of a learner's mastery of the content. They are only one piece. Following are some examples of objective assessment questions:

1. What are the three pillars of digital civics and citizenship?

   • educate, respect, and advocate (correct answer)
   • educate, respect, and love
   • educate, retrain, and advocate
   • educate, advocate, and train

2. Which of the following philosophical schools influences digital civics and citizenship?

   • Stoicism
   • Confucianism
   • nihilism
   • 1 and 2 (correct answer)

3. Are digital civics and citizenship education and practice founded on traditional civics and citizenship?

- Yes (correct answer)
- No

It is evident that these questions, while perfectly good to assess general knowledge, do not reach to the depths of understanding that a topic like digital civics and citizenship requires to display mastery. Given the nature of the topic, a more comprehensive means of measurement is required to authentically identify learners' mastery. For this reason, digital civics and citizenship is best measured using a combination of products and assessments. Combining these provides a better measurement to inform how learners and instructors should navigate the content and implement the practices in a more authentic way. The next section examines some recommended ways of combining products and assessments for successfully teaching and measuring mastery in digital civics and citizenship.

BLENDING PRODUCTS AND ASSESSMENTS

Striking a balance between products and assessments is something of a Sisyphean feat to accomplish in any education setting. However, it can be done and done successfully. In this section, a sample provides a point of reference for implementing digital civics and citizenship learning and practice.

The key to successfully blending products and assessments to achieve an authentic measurement is to keep the components varied and interesting. This is easily achieved by making sure that content knowledge and skills are not unnecessarily repeated in the products and assessments. In other words, if a concept, practice, or skill has already been measured in a traditional assessment, it should be avoided if possible in a product. However, if it is necessary that the concept or skill be used or incorporated into the product in order to achieve the expected outcome, then it must be repeated. It is recommended that the repeated measurement piece not be too obvious. Here's an example of what *not* to do:

Assessment: Define the term *civic virtue*.
Product: Include in your world cloud the definition of *civic virtue*.

While both of these measurement pieces, taken separately, are viable for use in measuring learners' mastery of understanding the term *civic virtue*, using both is redundant. Even though this may seem like an overly simple guideline to follow when creating measurements, it is one that is easily overlooked even by the most seasoned educators. As with most aspects of teaching and learning, diligence helps overcome this challenge.

Measuring learners' mastery regarding the definition of a crucial term is important. It is not something that should be sidelined in order to assess a concept or skill in a more complex manner for the sake of complexity. This is a trap that many educators easily fall into, so much so that it morphs into a regular practice. There is a simple two-step process that can help to avoid this pitfall when creating measurements. The two aspects of this process are authenticity and repetition.

AUTHENTICITY

Authenticity is the key factor in teaching and learning. Students in any context can quickly identify a teacher who does not believe in or see the importance of what they are teaching. Basically, if the teacher or the organization does not see the importance of what's being taught past a standardized test, the students are not likely to put much effort into learning and mastering the content and skills.

The concept of authenticity is not new and continues to receive renewed interest from educators. Former president Theodore Roosevelt summed it up well when he said, "Nobody cares how much you know until they know how much you care."[3] This crucial understanding has been spread by the writer John C. Maxwell, who writes on personal growth and leadership development. Maxwell makes this adage a cornerstone of his teachings. This is one of the facets of personal growth and leadership development that translates easily into teaching and learning. In fact, it is vital in all aspects of education.

One way of building authenticity within a learning experience and environment is by using the dual PBL system. PBL refers to either "problem-based learning" or "project-based learning," or to both. The first is the more recognized meaning. However, both approaches use content knowledge and skills from a course to address a real-world issue. The very nature of digital civics and citizenship lends itself to PBL to measure learners' mastery of the content. For our work here, the two PBL methods are differentiated by the perspective used. This was explored in more depth in chapter 11.

For example, problem-based learning looks to address and hopefully solve a problem that a community or individual is grappling with. Medical case studies are closely related to problem-based learning. An example of this is a patient presenting peculiar symptoms that may or may not be life-threatening. PBL would address diagnosing and treating the patient. In this sense, this PBL is reactive. There is a problem, and it must be solved.

On the other hand, project-based learning is proactive. In a certain sense, project-based learning builds from problem-based learning. Continuing with the medical example, once the initial patient is diagnosed and treated, the medical team can begin developing a treatment and prevention protocol for future use. Here are two examples of PBL for digital civics and citizenship, one for each method.

PROBLEM-BASED LEARNING

One of the continuing problems many individuals grapple with online is cyberbullying in all of its many forms. These include catfishing, gaslighting, and many others. For this learning experience, identify reasons why individuals may become victims of cyberbullying as well as why people perpetrate it. This learning experience does not necessarily look to assign blame but rather leads learners to identify the responsibilities of all parties involved.

From this point, the experience guides learners to examine different situations to identify how cyberbullying can be avoided. Students will pinpoint areas where individuals' awareness or understanding of digital civics and citizenship has gaps that may result in acts of cyberbullying. The instructor will help the learners analyze their findings and select the best method of communicating them.

PROJECT-BASED LEARNING

For digital civics and citizenship, project-based learning can be understood as something of a follow-up to problem-based learning with the reactive-proactive dichotomy already mentioned. For application in a learning experience, problem-based learning functions to mitigate the effects of a problem already studied and analyzed.

This second step offers a process to examine and analyze ways of adapting to a situation before it grows into a possible problem. For example, continuing with cyberbullying, students can explore and analyze means of circumventing acts of cyberbullying before they even occur. Solutions such as peer mentoring, formal and informal education programs, and self-governance can be explored and experimentally implemented in controlled environments in project-based learning.

As with problem-based learning, the instructor serves more as a guide in assisting learners with identifying possible solutions, experimentation, and communicating results. Some of the possible products from employing this method in teaching and learning digital civics and citizenship include the following:

- formal and community education programs
- after-school and summer programs
- community users groups
- community charters and constitutions

START AT THE END

Teaching is like any other professional project. An individual must begin with an acute understanding of what the end goal is, how it will be measured, and how completion will be identified. In fact, the same is true of learning. Students need to know what they are expected to learn as well as how they will be assessed in showing mastery. In other words, it's always best to begin with the end in mind for teaching and learning.

In regard to digital civics and citizenship, there are some unique challenges that present themselves to both instructors and learners. Regardless of the context (e.g., K–12, higher education, or community education), learners should have a sense of value in what they are learning. In a traditional approach, the content learned leads not only to passing a certain exam and matriculating to the next level of learning (i.e., grade level), but ultimately to graduation from the overall learning experience. Given the experiential nature of digital civics and citizenship, perspectives must be adjusted and re-oriented to a certain extent.

As examined earlier, learners can be assessed on their knowledge and comprehension of basic digital civics and citizenship content. This could include the history of civics and citizenship; the philosophies, beliefs, and attitudes that inform it; and some of the more agreed-upon practices. However, knowing and understanding are two different things.

Exhibiting these attitudes, beliefs, and practices is a sure way to measure a learner's mastery. As a result, scenario-based assessments and practices are the current best tool.

Previously the pedagogy and practice of using both problem-based and project-based assessments in the learning experience has been explored. In keeping with the beginning-with-the-end mind-set, sometimes referred to as reverse engineering, a digital civics and citizenship learning experience could also end with an online discussion or sharing with the group. The greatest challenge with measurements and assessments in digital civics and citizenship is authenticity.

This facet has already been explored in greater depth earlier in the chapter. However, that examination of authenticity in measurements and assessments was primarily focused on the student-facing portion. There is a need for authenticity in the instructor-facing aspect of this part of the learning experience. What this means is that the instructor must construct or adapt an assessment piece so that it has a workable balance of authenticity for both the learners and the instructor.

This means the instructor must create something new and unique that expressly addresses mastery or competency as the culmination of a planned learning experience. A good starting point for digital civics and citizenship instructors is to look at traditional assessments, such as questions on a test.

However, traditional assessments stop there. For digital civics and citizenship, it must be taken a step further. The experiential nature of digital civics and citizenship demands that the instructor look at traditional questions and ask, "What would this look like in practice?"

When an instructor can answer this question, they have an authentic assessment piece in front of them. From this piece, an authentic measurement of the learners' mastery and competency can be obtained. This begs the question of what this would look like in a learning environment or experience. As with most aspects of teaching and learning, there is not a set formula or recipe that an educator can follow and just plug in the pieces. Unfortunately, this is just the nature of teaching and learning.

Digital civics and citizenship teaching and learning are at their core experiential in nature. As such, measuring students' mastery of the content knowledge and skills must match the reality in which they operate on a daily basis. This means authentic assessments and products.

These two distinct tools used to measure learning must match not only what has been taught but also how the knowledge and skills are applied outside of the learning experience. Otherwise, the knowledge and skills will not be practiced outside of that learning experience.

When looking at ways of measuring learners' mastery of digital civics and citizenship skills and competency, designing products and assessments must be an early step in the development and design process. This aspect was examined more in depth in an earlier chapter. It is recommended that "beginning with the end in mind" is a sure way to cultivate success in learning digital civics and citizenship.

NOTES

1. https://eric.ed.gov/?id=ED380910.
2. Benjamin S. Bloom et al., *Taxonomy of Educational Objectives: The Classification of Educational Goals* (New York: McKay, 1956).
3. https://www.franklincovey.com/the-7-habits/habit-2.html.

Chapter Eighteen

Cultivating Culture

The term *culture* has become a buzzword among marketing and business professionals. For our purposes here, we understand culture as characteristics and knowledge of a particular group of people. This definition has also been adapted to mean the attitudes and practices within a business or organization. As a result, reevaluating a learning organization's culture has become a new focus in teaching and learning, as well as in educational administration. Peter Drucker, considered by many in business to be the guru of management, once admonished, "Culture eats strategy for breakfast," in his foundational work, *The Practice of Management*.[1]

More and more organizations are paying attention to and allocating funds for cultivating positive and productive cultures in their workplaces. Education is just starting to look at these practices and seeing how they can be not only adopted but successfully adapted. Teaching digital civics and citizenship is a powerful means of creating a positive and productive culture in a learning environment.

By its very nature, digital civics and citizenship places a premium on creating, cultivating, and communicating a positive and supportive culture among its practitioners. As explored in earlier chapters, digital civics and citizenship teaching and learning borrows heavily from traditional civics and citizenship education. Attitudes, behaviors, and actions that are practices of digital civics and citizenship are founded on education, respect, and advocacy.

While building culture presents challenges in any organization, there are unique characteristics of organizational culture that an educational setting must identify and weigh. The two primary facets of educational organizational culture are hierarchy and participation, or "buy-in." While both of these areas are similar to challenges in business and industrial organizations, they have a distinctive flavor in an educational setting. The next sections of this chapter establish a shared understanding of both and examine their importance.

HIERARCHY

According to clinical psychologist Jordan Peterson, hierarchies are biological. Some species of animals naturally organize themselves into hierarchies.[2] Instead of trying to dismantle this biological imperative, educators and learners can use it to their advantage. The key is orienting the point of view of leaders so that they understand that a major part of their responsibility is the people whom they lead. This is not to be misunderstood as a softer or gentler approach to leadership. Good leaders neither eat nor serve milquetoast. Hierarchies are constructs for building future leaders as well as for ensuring that there are stopgaps in place so that individuals do not slip by easily.

However, there are centuries of misuse or disuse of the concept of hierarchy that have attached negative connotations to it. Given the fact that the idea and practice of formal education have their roots in the medieval period in Western civilization, and even further back in many Eastern cultures, there are some practices and perspectives that require updating—or even upending—to now teach digital civics and citizenship authentically.

For example, the principal or headmaster of a school is a position that garners a certain amount of deference and respect, even if given grudgingly, simply due to the position itself.

Similarly, traditional classroom teachers have been provided a certain amount of professional respect due to their station within the organization. This is what is commonly referred to as positional authority.[3] However, this authority must be tempered with a certain amount of humility and openness by the individual holding the position. For example, principals at elementary schools often display this trait of openness and humility toward students. In this way, they model these character traits for the students, who are learning subconsciously.

K–20 schools are not going to abolish their hierarchies anytime soon. Given the fact that it is during these formative years of formal education that our worldview and understanding is established, many of our attitudes and behaviors toward learning are formed and carried into adulthood. This includes an understanding of the hierarchy in a learning environment, that is, the relationship between students, teachers, and administrators. So, instead of tearing down this established hierarchy, perhaps a better approach is to modify it through different practices.

As with any practice involving individuals, there is not a set process or standard protocol for achieving a flexible or fluid hierarchy in a learning environment. For some guidance in creating a flexible and flourishing hierarchy in a learning environment, the best example to build on comes from Plato. His idea, or ideal, of a philosopher king is something that students, teachers, and administrators can aspire to, within reason.[4] History provides evidence that Aristotle attempted to groom Alexander into a philosopher king, without much success. Thus, the need to temper the ideal with a realistic point of view is crucial.

One of the characteristics of a philosopher king, according to Plato, is that of the ruling individual being enlightened. While there are no real quantifiable measurements for identifying whether someone is enlightened, others can observe the quality that an individual in a leadership role is open to learning. This means that the individual in a leadership role must be open to guidance, including corrective guidance, to truly be open to learning. In other words, leaders of all stripes must be open enough to accept criticism from those they are responsible for, as well as asking for insight and guidance to make the situation better.

Added to this openness and flexibility in the traditional hierarchy, the practice of situational leadership is essential. Situational leadership provides all individuals, especially students, with the opportunity to operate in a leadership role. By doing this, individuals are provided with greater opportunity to educate, advocate for, and respect their peers. Remember, these three actions are the foundation upon which the teaching and learning of digital civics and citizenship resides. A traditional leadership hierarchy must be aware of situational leadership possibilities and opportunities. In an unhealthy environment, situational leadership can easily be taken advantage of. Many hands lighten the load, but everyone must carry their fair share of the responsibility of leadership. The following are a few examples of what this might look like in a traditional learning environment.

Example 1

After a virtual faculty meeting, a teacher discusses one-on-one with their administrator, who was facilitating the meeting, a reply given to another teacher's question. The teacher might share that they believed the response did not adequately address the question, or perhaps that it was harsh in tone. This takes courage, and it directly addresses the *advocacy* and *respect* portions of digital civics and citizenship.

Example 2

Working in a digital discussion board for a class assignment, a student witnesses exchanges between two other students that can be considered cyberbullying. Even though this student is friendly with both of the other students, they post a message to the two students explaining the danger in their posts. In doing this, the student is exercising all three of the facets of digital civics and citizenship: education, advocacy, and respect. While this is not an easy task, it is part of the civic virtue and *eudaimonia* explored in earlier chapters.

Example 3

An administrator witnesses students congregating. Upon further investigation, the administrator finds that the students are passing around explicit pictures of a fellow student on social media. Capitalizing on the opportunity, the administrator discusses the dangers of this kind of activity with the students, how seemingly simple exchanges that appear to be fun can objectify a person and hurt them emotionally and psychologically in their future friendships and relationships. The administrator also follows up with the student who was in the pictures. Perhaps ironically, some of the more traditional phrases used at times to scold someone still hold true. Some adults can recall being reprimanded, especially in school, and being asked rhetorical questions such as the following:

• What would your parents say/think?
• Would you say something like that to your mother/father/grandmother?
• When is it ever appropriate to say/do something like that?

Of course educators must be careful if and when they institute such phrases when correcting behaviors. And sadly, given the diversity of domestic experiences learners have nowadays, referencing a family member does not always hold the weight it used to. This does not mean that guidelines founded in these traditional remonstrances cannot be generated. Instructors and administrators should refine their professional lives for students in order to show and receive respect. Poise, deportment, and behavior communicating this mind-set are quickly noticed and picked up by learners. This does not mean that administrators and instructors should come off as cold, unapproachable, and disinterested. We are all human. Yet when students see us putting forward our best selves, they will come to emulate it as well as expect it from us.

Each of these examples shows a fluidity of leadership responsibilities taken by individuals, some of whom might not be considered traditional leaders. However, according to the theory of situational leadership, these individuals are leveraging their knowledge and skills at an opportune moment.[5] The fundamental skills and core knowledge of digital civics and citizenship are present in the resolution of each example. These examples show the necessity of a flexible and open hierarchy in a learning environment as well as the universal nature of some of the knowledge and skills learned and practiced in digital civics and citizenship.

Yet this flexible and open hierarchy coupled with situational leadership is not enough to cultivate a culture conducive to digital civics and citizenship teaching and learning. More is needed. For this model of leadership to work authentically and for digital civics and citizenship to be sincerely taught and learned, there must be buy-in from all faculty and staff in the learning environment. Just as in any other professional environment, and perhaps more so, the faculty and staff in a learning organization must sincerely believe in what they are teaching through consistent practice.

BUY-IN

Anytime there is a major shift, pivot, or change in an organization, obtaining buy-in from the individuals who compose the organization is paramount to success. This is especially true when there are attempts to change the culture of the organization. It is no different in a learning environment. Regardless of the context, the learning leader must not just embrace but also emanate the new culture. In a certain sense, instructors operate as cultural ambassadors to the students and to any visitors to the learning environment. Additionally, teachers in a digital civics and citizenship culture support one another in their behaviors and actions.

In the case of digital civics and citizenship, a distinct challenge faces administrators and instructors who want to educate learners in this set of knowledge and skills. Usually addressing cultural change in a professional environment focuses on leadership and grassroots efforts meeting in the middle to form something of a coalition for change. Some professional environments may leverage employment to implemental cultural change. In other words, leaders may implement changes, and if an employee refuses to comply, they can be summarily dismissed from the organization. It's not so easy in an educational setting.

Like cultural change in many other professional settings, adopting a culture of digital civics and citizenship in a learning organization is a combination of top-down and bottom-up efforts of the individuals who make up the organization. Given the very nature of digital civics and citizenship, the adoption of the curriculum and instruction should be as democratic a process as possible. This lays the foundation for authentic buy-in from faculty and staff. One of the key components in making this shift is communication. In fact, communication is part of the foundation of any culture. Shifting communication in a professional environment from a top-down construct to a more flattened practice is crucial in developing a culture that not only embraces but authentically practices and lives the principles of digital civics and citizenship.

However, the buy-in should not be difficult in a learning environment. Given the historical roots of formal education, practicing respect and advocacy along with education is a natural fit in a learning organization. By adopting the teaching of a digital civics and citizenship curriculum, learning organizations in some ways are taking back their historical perspective. Traditional civics and citizenship education was once a cornerstone of K–12 education in the United States and other nations. Over time, the focus has shifted away from civics and citizenship. This shift was examined in more detail in previous chapters.

The developmental theories and pedagogy behind these actions are solid. There is no disputing their effectiveness. However, as with any new curriculum or methodology, educators need to make some adjustments before adoption can take place. So, what does cultivating a culture for teaching and learning digital civics and citizenship look like in a classroom, on a campus, or in any learning organization? This is an honest question. While there is no clear-cut answer that can be dropped into place, looking back at traditional K–12 education, particularly at high school education in the United States, might provide a guide for implementing a digital civics and citizenship curriculum.

APPLICATION

Ironically, the curriculum and methodology that can perhaps best guide and inform digital civics and citizenship teaching and learning is almost nonexistent in secondary public education in the United States nowadays. It's driver's education. Yes, learning to operate a motor vehicle legally and responsibly shares quite a lot with digital civics and citizenship education.

Before wholly dismissing the idea, consider how most Gen Xers learned to drive versus how most millennials and younger generations learned. Most Gen Xers sat in a classroom and read through a very dry publication chockfull of the rules, ordinances, and laws of the road for their respective state. Only after showing mastery by passing the state written test and earning a driver's permit were they allowed to enroll in the actual driving portion of the course. Also, unlike other courses in high school, students had to pay to take this course regardless of the outcome. This provided an additional incentive to be successful.

One of the first lessons imprinted upon novice drivers is respect. They are taught respect for the road, for other drivers, and for the vehicle they are operating. In some instances, the driver's education teacher impresses the importance of respect for a vehicle by referring to it as a weapon. This is not a far stretch since automobile collisions too often result in permanent injury or death. Evidence shows that the same can be said of digital devices.

The respect taught in driver's education was based on safety. A driver was taught to be responsible for their vehicle, for their passengers, and for all with whom they shared the road. In a certain sense, driver's education, as well as driving itself, was the first time that many teenagers chose to take on adult responsibility. This exchange is a daily reminder, or at least it should be, that respect is a crucial aspect of our lives that is strengthened more when it is given rather than when it is expected or demanded.

Every time someone logs onto the internet, opens an app, or even sends an email, they are doing something very similar. However, there is little preparation for this responsibility. This realization brings us back to the question that spurred this text: What can be done to prepare individuals to responsibly use the internet and interact with one another in the digital sphere? Like driver's ed, participants in digital civics and citizenship education need to understand that respect is paramount—not only respect for their fellow citizens in the digital sphere, but also respect for the technology being used. Like an automobile, digital technology can be lethal.

Again, the answer offered in this text is, "Teach and practice digital civics and citizenship." Building from the framework provided by traditional driver's education methods and pedagogy, this new curriculum can objectively teach the practice of mutual respect. From this teaching and learning, the practice of mutual respect, similar to what was traditionally taught in driver's education, can lead to the practice of advocacy. From actions of mutual respect, where there is an objective respect for another individual, the practice of advocacy is a natural progression. An individual who respects another will advocate for that individual in times of crisis or conflict, regardless of the scale.

Building and transforming culture in any organization is a challenge, and often a difficult one. It requires that many of the individuals who make up the organization not only believe in the undertaking but also support it consistently through their behaviors and actions. When they do, the change in culture can not only be authentic but will also endure through personnel changes. Culture change like this is organic and nurturing for the organization.

For a learning organization, the key factor in adopting a culture that supports and nurtures digital civics and citizenship education is openness to learning. This seems like a nonissue when working with and in a learning organization. However, it is a common habit that most individuals, especially adults, fall into the trap of thinking that once their schooling is complete, they are done learning. For the same reason, professional development in most organizations is a challenge as well.

However, regarding digital civics and citizenship, this cultural shift is based on an inherent respect for all individuals within the organization. For Western-style democracies, this respect is part of the foundation of a representative government and a democratic, civil society. This respect, and by default the culture, requires daily nurturing that includes not just tending to its growth but also pruning bad habits. This builds so-called muscle memory so that these behaviors become habitual and automatic. As a result, the cyberworld behaviors and actions taught in digital civics and citizenship education are enacted in everyday exchanges, regardless of the context.

NOTES

1. Peter Drucker, *The Practice of Management* (New York: Harper & Row, 1954).

2. Jordan B. Peterson, *Maps of Meaning: The Architecture of Belief* (London: Routledge, 1999).

3. https://www.pmi.org/learning/library/influencing-without-authority-project-requirements-8100?id=8100.

4. Plato, *Republic*, trans. Robin Waterfield (Oxford: Oxford University Press, 1993).

5. Paul Hersey and Kenneth H. Blanchard, *Management of Organizational Behavior: Utilizing Human Resources*, 3rd ed. (Englewood Cliffs, NJ: Prentice Hall, 1977).

Chapter Nineteen

Looking Ahead

Prognostication and fortune-telling are fascinating ploys when it comes to pulling possible predictions out of thin air as a sideshow attraction at a carnival. They are, however, tricky skills to pull off when trying to make sincere forecasts in any endeavor involving humans. So, looking forward to the possible future of digital civics and citizenship education is debatable at best. Nevertheless, this final chapter attempts to look at trends and make recommendations for implementation and adaptation of digital civics and citizenship education in the years to come. While the specifics of the future of education at all levels is unclear, it is understood that including digital civics and citizenship in this future is essential in order to educate the whole learner.

From my own perspective and experience, there are two primary facets of education that will continue to influence and impact the development and practice of digital civics and citizenship, as well as all educational programs. These two facets are high-stakes testing and the future of teaching and learning. While these may seem broad and amorphous, they are crucial to consider in terms of how they may provide either a greater opportunity for or a larger challenge to implementation of digital civics and citizenship education.

Time is at the root of both facets. As with most anything in life, there rarely seems to be enough time to accomplish the necessities, let alone indulge in desired opportunities. This same situation exists within learning experiences, especially in formal settings. In the United States, K–12 students have hundreds of standards to master, along with huge amounts of knowledge and skills to become competent in, all within the span of less than two hundred school days each year. On top of this, teachers also have the challenge of differentiating the learning experiences in order to best provide learning that best suits the students. It's dizzying when anyone steps back and considers it from a larger perspective. Nonetheless, the vast majority of students are successful, at least according to standardized measures and assessments.

Attempting to load additional standards into any of the core subjects of math, English, science, and social studies rouses rebellious cries from educators. Similarly, attempting to squeeze additional subjects into the curriculum is doubly challenging. Already in this text, we've explored ways of embedding digital civics and citizenship into the core subject areas in K–12 education. Doing so in higher education is similar. However, both higher and community education provide platforms for stand-alone courses and learning experiences in digital civics and citizenship. K–12 education is where the greatest challenges lie.

Given the pandemic experience with which the world continues to grapple, challenges like social distancing and remote learning will continue to change the nature of formal education. They must. As a result, many students and teachers are finding that they can achieve the same or similar results in less time. Similarly, transferring in-person teaching and learning to a digital experience also continues to reveal the knowledge and skills gaps that digital civics and citizenship education can help to address.

This convergence of events and factors in teaching and learning, while creating some new stresses for students and teachers, may just prove to be the "golden ticket" opportunity that digital civics and citizenship needs and deserves. Similarly, the ubiquitous nature of technology demands that users have the knowledge and tools necessary for communicating and just existing in the digital sphere. With this understanding, digital civics and citizenship moves from a fringe elective curriculum solidly into the core of K–12 education.

By its very nature, digital civics and citizenship education is ready-made for online teaching and learning. In fact, this may be the best place for its teaching and learning to begin. Whether it's in K–12, higher education, or community education, teaching digital civics and citizenship online is the surest way to engage students and reveal immediate authenticity to the overall learning experience. Doing so provides access to an immersive experience for learners. Immersive learning has been shown in research to be one of the most effective ways to learn almost anything.

The predominant shift that needs to occur in education to provide digital civics and citizenship an entrée into the core curriculum is a decreased focus on standardized, high-stakes testing. An increasing amount of research reveals that these tests, and the continued hyperfocus on them, not only create undue anxiety for students and teachers but also do not provide an accurate or equitable measure of either learning or teaching.

Even though in the United States almost half of the states require graduating high school students to successfully pass a test that mirrors the civics portion of the naturalization test administered to immigrants by the federal government, this test is not necessarily a good measure of civics and citizenship knowledge, digital or otherwise. The test itself is based on low-level knowledge and comprehension questions, according to Bloom's taxonomy. This is just the foundation of civics and citizenship literacy. In digital civics and citizenship, the majority of the comprehension and practice is based on behaviors and actions. It is good for learners to understand the reasoning behind these behaviors and actions, as well as their possible effects.

However, these are not skills that can be completely or accurately measured by a traditional exam. Chapter 18 of this text explores measurements and assessments and offers recommendations for adapting traditional exams. Since standardized testing has been allowed to grow into its own industry, eradicating it will not be quick and may not be complete. In some ways, these measurements are necessary to build a framework to understand a learner's competencies and deficiencies. Yet using these assessments as complete and stand-alone mechanisms to measure learners' progress is insufficient. Adding other measurements to this testing, such as portfolios highlighting exemplars of learners' work, provides a more rounded picture of an individual's educational accomplishments.

Educational delivery and standardized tests aside, there is a deeper issue at hand regarding the teaching and learning of digital civics and citizenship. Learners for decades, at least in the US public education system, have been offered a shallow education. For example, beginning in elementary school science classes, students learn the steps of the scientific method. This knowledge is continually retaught throughout their educational experience, including high school. However, rarely if ever do students examine why this method is used in scientific research. The scientific method's importance, evolution, and even the consequences of its misuse are not topics found couched in learning standards in any state of the United States.

In other words, learners are being taught *how* to do science, but not necessarily *why* science should be done. There is little if any exploration or practice of scientific thinking. Similarly, students are not taught or given the opportunity to practice looking at and engaging with our world as a scientist would. As such, learners come to understand science in its capacity as a tool but not its role as a philosophy. This is dangerous not only for the students and teachers involved but for the world as a whole. In fact, one could argue that this type of industrialized education borders on being criminal.

One of the best ways to guide and assist this behavioral and practical shift in education is to keep instructors learning as well. Admittedly, K–12 teachers are required to complete a certain amount of professional development each year as part of maintaining their certification. Teachers usually spend the majority of their summers engaged in this way. However, there is little teacher-led professional development, especially during the scheduled school year. Since evidence shows that students learn from the practice of their teachers, it makes sense that having regular professional development throughout the academic year is called for.

One way to address this need in an organic and teacher-led fashion is to adopt professional learning communities (PLCs).[1] These teacher-led small groups provide an opportunity for educators to explore the latest research, best practices, and recent discoveries, as well as more local matters pertaining to their students. The very nature of these groups and their practices creates opportunities not only to learn more about digital civics and citizenship and to refine teaching pedagogy for this content, but also to practice its precepts among peers.

PLCs are a safe place for teachers to not only learn but also practice. Here, peers learn from each other as well as teach one another. It is a flat group where even the designated leader is only responsible for reporting back to administration the success of the group, nothing more. Leveraging this well-researched practice within the faculty of a learning organization ultimately assists students in being successful in all of their academic endeavors, including digital civics and citizenship. With just a little training and guidance, a learning organization can implement the practice of PLCs effectively.

The Reverend Dr. Martin Luther King Jr. summed up this dilemma well in a speech delivered at Morehouse College in 1948. In that speech, he said, "The function of education, therefore, is to teach one to think intensively and to think critically. But education which stops with efficiency may prove the greatest menace to society. The most dangerous criminal may be the man gifted with reason, but with no morals."[2] While this seems dire and even dangerous, the fruits of such a shallow or one-dimensional education fill the daily news in regard to political statements and other occurrences that reveal a poor understanding of the workings of a democratic society.

This brings the discussion around to the core challenge of digital civics and citizenship education. Actually, it is the root problem with education as a whole, especially in the United States. In the *Dialogues of Plato*, Plato records many insightful and wise admonitions from his teacher Socrates.[3] One of these discussions involves the education of an individual, particularly a citizen of Athens. In this dialogue, Plato asserts that the end goal of education is the realization that one is mortal. From this realization, Plato continues, the conclusion arises that with this knowledge, individuals must ascertain how they can live their lives to be of the greatest benefit to themselves, their families, and society as a whole.[4]

Less than a century ago, the humanities were understood by society, especially in the United States, as helpful in educating the character of students. While this was not the only educational responsibility levied upon the humanities, it was a crucial one. A humanities education was understood to complement the moral and ethical instruction students were expected to receive from their parents and the larger society through religious organizations and social groups, such as scouting organizations. However, in the last half of the twentieth century, this began to fall apart in the United States.

The causes of this dissolution continue to be debated. It has also spurred the development of new educational and social initiatives. These include cultural literacy founded by E. D. Hirsch, iCivics, and even more individually focused initiatives. The most recent example is that of Dr. Jordan Peterson with his best-selling book *12 Rules for Life: An Antidote to Chaos.*[5] As a result of these initiatives, much debate and even conflict rages among scholars, educators, and individuals. While this may seem to be a lot of noise about nothing, it is actually very important.

Embedding digital civics and citizenship education within the established curriculum in a learning organization is not only a powerful way of bringing the humanities to the forefront of teaching and learning but can also breathe new life into this curricular area. Given the fact that at their root the humanities strive to guide learners in answering the question of what it means to be human and to live in a human society, practicing the tenets of digital civics and citizenship allows learners not only to grapple with these ageless questions but to look to those who have done so before and added a piece to the solution.

In fact, digital civics and citizenship helps to answer a seemingly more pressing question: Why do I have to learn this? This is commonly asked by students when reading a novel, watching a play, listening to a piece of music, or looking at a particular piece of art. So very often, even in our own experiences, no easy or concise answer is given. Yet, through digital civics and citizenship, a framework of an answer is possible. Instead of being told that it's on the test or it's part of the course, students can be answered that "this will help you understand what it means to be human and to live among fellow humans."

With this understanding, digital civics and citizenship education can be seen as a humanizing agent within the ever more chilling practice of education. The overt focus on data, such as scores, grades, and attendance—necessary and helpful tools—has seemingly removed the heart and soul from the classroom. Digital civics and citizenship provides a means for exploring and practicing human relationships through digital technology so that learners connect what they are practicing to the real world. Like learning experiences in a laboratory science or performing arts class, digital civics and citizenship education not only opens the learners to deeper and more authentic communication using technology, but also provides the opportunity to practice for the real, larger world outside of the learning environment.

In the midst of the debates over the future of education, online learning, and even the future of humanities education stands digital civics and citizenship. The learning and practice of the knowledge and skills found in digital civics and citizenship begins to address the issues framed by these debates. The ideas and behaviors anchored in responsibility, respect, and advocacy are applied in real-world settings so that learners are experienced and practiced in navigating the digital sphere successfully and safely.

The Irish playwright George Bernard Shaw once said, "Some men see things as they are and ask why. Others dream things that never were and ask why not."[6] This point of view was made popular in the 1960s by the Kennedy brothers. John F. Kennedy, while president, used this quote in a speech to the Parliament of Ireland. Later, his brother, Robert F. Kennedy, paraphrased it in one of his presidential campaign speeches. Regarding digital civics and citizenship education, it is apropos to use when faced with the eternal question of *why*.

When debating the value, adoption, and implementation of digital civics and citizenship education within a community, *why* is an ever-present question. Drawing support from daily headlines regarding cyberbullying, cybercrime, and exploitation, especially of minors, on the internet, perhaps the best rebuttal is to ask, Why not? What community does not want to teach and practice respect, advocacy, and education to all of its members, or at least provide its constituent members with the opportunities to learn and practice these informed behaviors?

Just as important as the decision to teach and practice digital civics and citizenship in a community is the realization that this undertaking is not a cure-all. Teaching and practicing the actions and behaviors of digital civics and citizenship will not produce an immediate reduction in cyberbullying or cybercrime. It will not immediately impact the overall crime rate in a community. Teaching digital civics and citizenship is not a preventive measure, per se. Rather, it is an ongoing act of preparation.

To put this understanding metaphorically, the British writer and theologian G. K. Chesterton once said,

> Fairy tales, then, are not responsible for producing in children fear, or any of the shapes of fear; fairy tales do not give the child the idea of the evil or the ugly; that is in the child already, because it is in the world already. Fairy tales do not give the child his first idea of bogey. What fairy tales give the child is his first clear idea of the possible defeat of bogey. The baby has known the dragon intimately ever since he had an imagination. What the fairy tale provides for him is a St. George to kill the dragon. Exactly what the fairy tale does is this: it accustoms him for a series of clear pictures to the idea that these limitless terrors had a limit, that these shapeless enemies have enemies in the knights of God, that there is something in the universe more mystical than darkness, and stronger than strong fear.[7]

So, with this understanding, the purpose of digital civics and citizenship education is not necessarily to prevent individuals from encountering predators online, or even from becoming predators themselves. Rather it is to prepare them for these encounters and equip them with the knowledge and skills to successfully overcome these situations and defeat the predators who roam around the digital sphere. So the challenge is for each of us to do what we can to incorporate digital civics and citizenship education where we are, to the extent that we can. Doing this and adding our voices to the call for its incorporation into the PK–20 curriculum, as well as in community education, will help to challenge us all to be better citizens of the global community.

NOTES

1. Richard DuFour and Robert Eaker, *Professional Learning Communities at Work: Best Practices for Enhancing Student Achievement* (Bloomington, IN: Solution Tree, 1998).

2. https://projects.seattletimes.com/mlk/words-education.html.

3. B. Jowett, trans., *The Dialogues of Plato* (New York: Scribner, 1911).

4. Jowett, *The Dialogues of Plato*.

5. Jordan B. Peterson, *12 Rules for Life: An Antidote to Chaos* (Toronto: Random House Canada, 2018).

6. George Bernard Shaw, *Back to Methuselah*, in *Selected Plays with Prefaces*, 2:7 (New York: Dodd, Mead, 1949).

7. G. K. Chesterton, "The Red Angel," in *Tremendous Trifles* (New York: Dodd, Mead, 1909).

Resources

WEBSITES

http://digitalcivics.org
https://www.coe.int/en/web/digital-citizenship-education/digital-citizenship-and-digital-citizenship-education
https://digitalcivics.io
https://www.commonsense.org/education/digital-citizenship
https://digcitutah.com/digital-citizenship
https://www.cybercivics.com/free-digital-citizenship-course
https://pz.harvard.edu/resources/digital-civics-toolkit
https://www.cyberwise.org/digital-citizenship-resources
https://www.iea.nl/studies/iea/iccs
https://www.foundry10.org/programs/digital-civics
https://www.digitalcitizenship.net/home.html
https://literacy.ala.org/digital-literacy/
https://www.alsc.ala.org/blog/2017/04/digital-citizenship-resources-librarians/
https://www.ed.gov/civic-learning

ARTICLES

https://interactions.acm.org/archive/view/july-august-2015/digital-civics
https://www.researchgate.net/publication/301521607_Digital_Civics_Citizen_Empowerment_With_and_Through_Technology
https://www.iste.org/explore/digital-citizenship/digital-citizenship-new-citizenship
https://www.sciencedirect.com/science/article/abs/pii/S0885985X13000697
https://oecdedutoday.com/citizenship-and-education-in-a-digital-world
https://www.rand.org/content/dam/rand/pubs/conf_proceedings/CF300/CF373/RAND_CF373.pdf
http://www.democracyreadyny.org/Developing-Digital-Citizens.pdf
https://apolitical.co/en/solution_article/the-digital-citizen-is-here-are-governments-ready
https://www.iste.org/explore/5-competencies-digital-citizenship
https://www.tolerance.org/frameworks/digital-literacy
https://www.digitalcitizenship.net/nine-elements.html

https://www.americanprogress.org/issues/education-k-12/reports/2018/02/21/446857/state-civics-education

BOOKS

Busch, Elizabeth Kaufer, and Jonathan W. White. *Civic Education and the Future of American Citizenship*. Lanham, MD: Lexington Books, 2013.

Graber, Diana. *Raising Humans in a Digital World: Helping Kids Build a Healthy Relationship with Technology*. New York: HarperCollins, 2019.

Mattson, Kristen. *Digital Citizenship in Action: Empowering Students to Engage*. Portland, OR: International Society for Technology in Education, 2017.

Mossberger, Karen, Caroline J. Tolbert, and Ramona S. McNeal. *Digital Citizenship: The Internet, Society, and Participation*. Cambridge, MA: MIT Press, 2007.

Ohler, Jason B. *Digital Community, Digital Citizen* (Thousand Oaks, CA: Corwin Press, 2010).

Ribble, Mike. *Digital Citizenship in Schools*. 2nd ed. Eugene, OR: International Society for Technology in Education, 2011.

Richardson, Janice Patricia, and Elizabeth Milovidov. *Digital Citizenship Education Handbook: Being Online, Well-Being Online, and Rights Online*. Hilton Strasbourg: Council of Europe, 2019.

Wells, Chris. *The Civic Organization and the Digital Citizen: Communicating Engagement in a Networked Age*. Oxford: Oxford University Press, 2015.

STANDARDS

https://www.socialstudies.org/standards/national-curriculum-standards-social-studies-introduction
https://www.socialstudies.org/standards/c3
https://www.nextgenscience.org

For institutions of higher learning, each region has its own accreditation agency that provides standards for different domains of learning. It is recommended that readers check with their local accreditation organization for specific information regarding civics and citizenship. For example, https://www.msche.org/standards. Similarly, other nongovernmental organizations (NGOs) provide standards for civics and citizenship as well. For example:

https://www.digitalcivics.org
https://www.digitalcivicstoolkit.org
https://ec.europa.eu/digital-single-market
https://openlab.ncl.ac.uk

Index

About the Author

Casey Davis is an instructional designer for the Watts College of Public Service and Community Solutions at Arizona State University. Prior to joining Watts College, he was an instructional designer at the University Technology Office at ASU. He previously worked for Pearson Education as a K–12 science curriculum specialist and was the senior curriculum manager for the humanities at Flip Switch. Prior to that he taught science, social studies, English, and journalism and was the secondary advanced academics facilitator for the Temple Independent School District for three years before returning to the classroom full time. Mr. Davis has been a contract writer for STEMscopes at Rice University as well as a freelance writer for SAGE Publications, ABC-Clio, and OnLine Learners. The tenth edition of his world history textbook *Exploring World History* (with ancillary materials) was published by the American Preparatory Institute. He has also written a book on secondary social studies classroom techniques titled *Social Studies Comes Alive!* and published by Prufrock Press.